Praise for *HeroZ*

"*HeroZ* is for everyone! Now workers and managers have their own magic arrow to penetrate the thick scales of hierarchy and tired, old thinking. *HeroZ* lights our way to actualizing what we already know in our hearts: teamwork and participation *are* the best ways to unleash potential and achieve organizational success!"

—Donald Romine
President, Web Industries, Inc.

"*HeroZ* utilizes metaphor to powerfully illustrate the importance of self-empowerment. The story brings to life the impact of Reengineering and Total Quality Management on workers, customers, and society. Most important, it's about taking ownership of our future."

—George E. Murray
Director, Quality Technologies Institute
Polaroid Corporation

"*HeroZ* makes it clear how personal empowerment, quality understanding, setting objectives, measurement, teamwork, and positive feedback lead to superior customer satisfaction—all in a very readable fable!"

—Bill Garwood
President, Tennessee Eastman Division
Eastman Chemical Company
1993 Winner of the Malcolm Baldridge Award

"I loved *HeroZ*! The most useful lesson for me was that I am ultimately in control of my success and failure—my destiny—and that I *can* influence others and impact the quality of our work!"

—Laurie Lack
Account Executive
Strategic Mortgage Services

Other books by
William C. Byham, Ph.D.

Zapp! The Lightning of Empowerment
with Jeff Cox

Zapp! in Education
with Jeff Cox and Kathy Harper Shomo

Zapp! Empowerment in Health Care
with Jeff Cox, Kathy Harper Shomo,
and Sharyn B. Materna

*Empowered Teams: Creating Self-directed
Work Groups That Improve Quality,
Productivity, and Participation*
with Richard S. Wellins and Jeanne M. Wilson

*Shogun Management: How North Americans
Can Thrive in Japanese Companies*
with George Dixon

*Leadership Trapeze: Strategies for Leadership
in Team-Based Organizations*
with Jeanne Wilson, Jill George, and
Richard Wellins

Assessment Centers and Managerial Performance
with George C. Thornton III

Other books by Jeff Cox

*The Quadrant Solution: A Business Novel That
Solves the Mystery of Sales Success*
with Howard Stevens

The Goal: A Process of Ongoing Improvement
with Eliyahu M. Goldratt

ᵀᴹ

Empower Yourself,
Your Coworkers,
Your Company

William C. Byham, Ph.D.,
and Jeff Cox

Fawcett Columbine • New York

A Fawcett Columbine Book
Published by Ballantine Books

Copyright © 1994 by William C. Byham, Ph.D., and Jeff Cox

HeroZ™ is a registered trademark of Development Dimensions International

http://www.randomhouse.com

This edition published by arrangement with Harmony Books, a division of Crown Publishers, Inc.

Library of Congress Catalog Card Number: 94-90787

ISBN: 0-449-90958-1

Manufactured in the United States of America
First Ballantine Books Edition: August 1995
10   9   8   7

To all of us who work for a living…
And especially the 700 worldwide associates
of Development Dimensions International,
who model on a daily basis the values of
empowerment, continuous improvement,
and dedication to customer service.
You are true HeroZ.

Acknowledgments

No one writes a book alone. Literally hundreds of people helped create the vision for this book—from associates at Development Dimensions International who work closely with organizations as they journey toward a more empowering culture to the vast number of readers who called or wrote to us after reading our first book, *Zapp! The Lightning of Empowerment.*

Many individuals made important contributions to this book by critiquing various drafts, offering ideas, and providing real-life examples from their personal experiences. Others worked diligently on the production, marketing, and promotion of the book.

• HeroZ from Development Dimensions International who deserve special recognition include Tammy Bercosky, Barbara Brumm, Jill Faircloth, Nancy Hrynkiw, Lee Kricher, Anne Maers, Holly Rudoy, and Carol Schuetz. Other DDI associates who assisted with the book include Dave Biber, Andrea Eger, Chuck Faber, Linda Francis, Shawn Garry, Shelby Gracey, Sandy Hilker, Diana Jannot, Jody Lange, Helene Lautman, Billie Nestor, Bill Proudfoot, Jamie Rondeau, and Kathy Harper Shomo. Special thanks to Pam Miller and Karen Munch for creating the HeroZ logo design.

• HeroZ from Crown Publishers and Harmony Books who deserve special recognition include Amy Boorstein, Cathy Collins, Joan DeMayo, Patty Eddy, John Fontana, John Groton, Peter Guzzardi, Sarah Hamlin, Steve Magnuson, Andy Martin, Pam Romano, Michelle Sidrane, Joy Sikorski, Penny Simon, Laurie Stark, Robin Strashun, and Helen Zimmermann.

Thank you for your ideas, encouragement, and hard work.

Years ago, when the world was more in awe of technology than it is now, a number of people predicted that machines of one type or another would someday do all the work unattended and that we human beings would enjoy an Age of Leisure. Life would be one very long vacation.

Of course, this has not come to pass and will not anytime soon. But this is probably just as well. For one thing, the predictors of the Age of Leisure were a little fuzzy on exactly how we would each pay for this life-long vacation, as we would not have jobs. But even more serious is the fact that we human beings need work to a greater degree than most of us like to admit.

The truth is that work gives us not only a paycheck, but a significant piece of our sense, as individuals, of who we are. Meet a stranger and the second or third bit of information this person usually wants to know about you (after your name and where you live) is what kind of work you do. As adults in this society, our work has a big influence on our self-esteem and our notions of self-worth, as anyone without a job is only too well aware.

One of the biggest issues we presently face is not what to do with all of our leisure time, but how to create new jobs, how to make the jobs we already have more productive in terms of value delivered, and how to get the world economy growing again. This is not just an issue for politicians and economists; it is an issue in which all of us have a role to play. And it is not just a matter of jobs and paychecks; we want those jobs in the end to make our country and our world a less trouble-ridden, more prosperous, more healthy, more enjoyable place to live. That is the ultimate meaning of good work.

HeroZ™ is a story about how to help that happen. It is a story about everyday people who take control of their jobs and relentlessly improve the way they work so that in the end everybody wins. Along the way, they have to keep learning—about measurements and goals, about how to interact with their coworkers and their boss, about working in teams, about problem solving and many other things. The energy that keeps them going is empowerment, what we call *Zapp!*

A few years ago, we wrote a book entitled *Zapp! The Lightning of Empowerment*. That was a story about how managers can empower their employees. *HeroZ*™ is a story about how employees can empower *themselves* and spread that empowerment to their coworkers and even to their boss.

Though written in story form, both *Zapp!* and

HeroZ™ are practical books. They are written as fables, because this form makes it possible to disregard the distracting differences between organizations and industries so that we can concentrate on the essentials. Also, we figured that a book written as a fable would be a heck of a lot more fun to read than a book written in typical textbook fashion. Yet within these stories, we give you not just an explanation of the idea of empowerment, but the step-by-step methods for actually making empowerment work.

Now, some people out there probably will claim that they don't care whether they are empowered or not. What difference does it make? Well, it does make a difference. First of all, the success of the organizations in our society determines our success as individuals. If they fail, we fail. On the other hand, if our organizations succeed and deliver high value to their customers, then this success is imparted to us as individuals in many tangible and intangible ways—money, quality goods and services to buy with that money, personal satisfaction, a meaningful life.

Empowerment is essential to making an organization successful on a continuing, long-term basis. In a fast-paced, ever-changing global economy, with more complexity than in the past, with heightened demands and expectations on the part of customers, the old organizational structures do not work very well. They can't react fast enough. These days, the organization that wishes to remain competitive needs more than a few heads at the top of the organization working on ways to improve performance. It needs the involvement of those working nearest to the customer and of those who are actually creating the value the customer is paying for. Empowerment is the best way to gain that involvement.

So empowerment is good for the organization, but what does it do for you, the individual? Until that long-awaited Age of Leisure arrives, or until you win the lottery, you probably need to work for a living, just like the rest of us. Will empowerment put more money in your pocket? Possibly, it may—though probably not immediately, but over the long haul, because gains in productivity make possible gains in wages. Certainly if you and your coworkers enable your organization to adapt successfully to the changing needs and demands of customers, this is also in your financial best interest. Continuous improvement enhances the likelihood of a continuing paycheck.

But should work just be about earning a wage? Isn't there more to life than money? We spend a huge portion of our lives at work. Why shouldn't that time be traded for more than just bucks and benefits? Why shouldn't work also be satisfying? Why shouldn't we also find a sense of meaning and fulfillment on the job? Why can't we look forward to going to work with as much anticipation as we look forward to weekends, holidays, and vacations?

Well, there are some people who do not wish for life to be just an endless weekend. Some people actually look forward to Monday mornings. Who are these folks? By and large, they are the empowered people. They are the ones who have control over their work, can make meaningful decisions, can measure their progress, and are considered valuable to their organizations and customers. If you are not yet among their ranks, you can be. Empowerment is a way for you to get more out of a very important part of your life: those hours you spend on the job.

Remember, of course, that a book of this length is not intended to be an encyclopedia on the subject. Remember also that it will take time, patience, and practice to empower yourself and the people around you, and that a book is not a substitute for training. But the fundamentals are within these pages. Based on thousands upon thousands of individuals who have learned about *Zapp!* and empowerment through training programs and who subsequently used them on the job, it is clear that the ideas in this book really work. If you apply them, you will create empowerment; you will reap benefits for customers you serve, for the people you work with, and for yourself.

William C. Byham, Ph.D., and Jeff Cox
Pittsburgh, Pennsylvania, USA, 1994

1

Once upon a time, in a magic land near you, there was a castle.

This was the famous Lamron Castle. It was a large castle with many towers and walls, and it was very important to the people of the countryside around it.

Because on any given day, from out of the sky, came dragons who had nothing better to do than cause problems and wreak havoc for anyone upon whom they descended.

For this reason, every household in Lamron kept a brass horn handy. Whenever a dragon came out of the sky, the threatened citizen was supposed to get on the horn—and then take cover and hide.

Alert lookouts on the walls of the castle, if they had not already spotted the dragon, would hear the sound of the horns and the castle would promptly dispatch a knight who would gallop to the rescue.

In exchange for this service, the castle charged a modest fee. But the citizens of Lamron were always happy to pay it because the dragons were nothing to mess with if you were not a trained professional.

You see, this was a magic universe and these dragons

were immortal. Really, they were impossible to kill.

Only knights could deal with dragons. Oh sure, once in a while some do-it-yourselfer would grab a sword and run out there, hacking and slashing at the attacking dragon—only to get himself cooked and eaten. Humans, unlike dragons, were very mortal.

But the knights could deal with the dragons because years ago the wise King of Lamron Castle had directed his wizards to develop a high-tech weapon: the Magic Arrow.

Upon arriving at the scene, the knight would charge—swerving left and right, dodging streams of fire breath, swipes of sharp claws, swishes of the dragon's scaly tail, and bites of jagged teeth—until close enough to shoot a Magic Arrow directly into the monster's heart.

Once struck in the heart with a Magic Arrow, the invading dragon would immediately begin to shrink—smaller and smaller and smaller—until, in a brilliant burst of light, the dragon would vanish completely, sent back to the parallel dimension from which it had come.

Whereupon the knight would present a bill to the citizen who had blown the horn, and ask, "Will this be cash, check, or charge?"

For a long while, this arrangement worked well for everybody.

With relief from havoc-wreaking dragons, life for the

Lamronian citizens became peaceful and the land became prosperous. And, much to the benefit of the local economy, the castle employed many of those from the surrounding countryside, who earned good pay and spent it freely. Times were good.

But times change.

Among those many from the surrounding countryside who worked at the Castle was Art Halegiver.

Art was not a knight. In fact, in all his years working at the castle, he'd never even seen a dragon up close. Art was an arrow-maker over in Tower Two. He was one of dozens upon dozens of people who toiled within the towers making the Magic Arrows and armor and other things the knights needed to keep the dragons at bay.

One day, like every day, Art was eating lunch in the castle courtyard with his two friends Mac and Wendy.

All three of them were arrow-makers in Tower Two, though they did different jobs.

Art was a shaft-turner. He turned out shafts for the arrows from sticks of wood brought in from the surrounding forests.

Mac was a head-shaper. That is, he shaped the arrow-heads, which were made from a special metal and had to be hammered to exact dimensions specified by castle wizards.

And Wendy was a wand-waver. Though she was not a wizard herself, she had her degree in Magical Sciences and was a licensed wand-waving practitioner. She and the other wand-wavers worked at the top of the Tower adding magic to the finished arrows that came from the lower floors.

The three of them had been friends for years, and they ate lunch together four out of five days a week.

So here this noon was Art, sitting with them, eating his tuna fish sandwich, staring at the castle wall, half listening to Wendy chatter away about her and her husband wallpapering their bedroom last weekend, and half wondering to himself why he didn't like his job.

Art hadn't always not liked his job. In the beginning, he had loved his job, at least on the better days. But in the last few years, his feelings had changed. In fact, there were often times when he even hated his job.

Hating his job didn't make any sense. Arrow-making was honest work and he was fairly good at it. And it paid okay money, which was mainly why he stayed. Outside the castle, good-paying jobs for shaft-turners were scarce in this magic land.

But hate his job he often did and he couldn't quite figure out why. In a little while, the three of them would go back to doing the same boring arrow-making work, which they always did the same way every day until it all got so dull nobody cared. Maybe that was it; maybe that was why Art didn't like his job.

Of course, he realized there was no use thinking about this for very long, because there was nothing to be done about it. He needed gold to pay his bills, and for gold he had to work. So Art Halegiver forced his whole mind to listen to Wendy describe the lovely floral pattern of her wallpaper.

"So what are you going to do *this* weekend?" Mac asked her. "Wallpaper the basement?"

"No, we're going to help Mom and Dad move," she said.

"How come they're moving?" asked Art. "Don't they like their wallpaper?"

"No, in fact, they don't have any wallpaper. Didn't I tell you? A dragon burned their house down."

"Oh. Gee, I'm sorry. That's too bad," said Art. "What happened? Didn't they get on the horn to the castle?"

"Sure they did," said Wendy. "But there were problems."

"What kind of problems?"

"Well, the knight came to the rescue a little late," said Wendy, "and when he did arrive, it seems that a number of our Magic Arrows just didn't work. The knight kept charging around, shooting at the heart, but the dragon didn't go away. So pretty soon, the knight ran out of arrows and had to gallop back to the castle for more. By the time he returned, the dragon had set their house on fire and Mom and Dad were about to be roasted for dinner. Luckily, the next arrow the knight shot hit the dragon's heart."

"Wow," said Art, "I guess your mom and dad were mad."

"Yes, they were. But the worst of it was the bill was so high that they almost wished the dragon had eaten them."

"So they're moving? Where are they going to go?" asked Mac.

"They're not sure, but they're definitely leaving Lamron," said Wendy.

"But they're sure to get burned if they don't stay in Lamron," said Mac. "We're the best castle around! We're the only ones with the Magic Arrows!"

"That's not what Dad says. He says he read in *Dragon Digest* that Lamron Castle is still the standard, but there are lots of new castles springing up just over the horizon that are offering guaranteed fast service and low, low prices."

"That's right," said Art. "Haven't you heard about Castle Colossal? Their knights use the new Smart Arrows that never miss."

"Well, what's wrong with us?" asked Mac. "How come our knights don't get there faster? How come our arrows don't work better? Why are our prices so high? Why isn't somebody *doing* something?"

Oddly enough, at almost the same moment, the King of Lamron Castle was asking almost exactly the same kinds of questions.

Herb's: Expose Yourself!   11.00
0446909581

SUB TOTAL   11.00
SALES TAX   .89
TOTAL   11.89

AMOUNT TENDERED

CASH   20.00

TOTAL PAYMENT   20.00
CHANGE   8.11

Full refund issued for new and unread books and unopened music within 30
days with a receipt from any Barnes & Noble store.

Store Credit issued for new and unread books and unopened music after 30
days or without a sales receipt. Credit issued at <u>lowest sale price</u>.

We gladly accept returns of new and unread books and unopened music from
bn.com with a bn.com receipt for store credit at the bn.com price.

Full refund issued for new and unread books and unopened music within 30
days with a receipt from any Barnes & Noble store.

Store Credit issued for new and unread books and unopened music after 30
days or without a sales receipt. Credit issued at <u>lowest sale price</u>.

We gladly accept returns of new and unread books and unopened music from
bn.com with a bn.com receipt for store credit at the bn.com price.

2

You see, that morning the King had decided to reward a knight who had done a particularly good deed.

So he went up to the Treasure Room, way up at the top of the King's Keep, to get a bag of gold.

But when he unlocked the treasure chest, he was shocked to see that the chest was nearly empty.

The King called together all his dukes and said, "Hey, what goes here? Where's all the gold that used to be in the chest?"

The dukes all silently shrugged their shoulders, all except the Duke of Accounting, who said, "Your Majesty, I'm afraid that lately we've been paying out more gold than we've been taking in."

"And just how did that happen?" asked the King.

"Well, Magic Arrows are not cheap to make, Sire, and the knights and the castle are very expensive to maintain—"

"I know that!" said the King. "Why aren't we taking in enough gold to cover the costs? Don't tell me that there aren't enough dragons to fight!"

"Oh, you betcha, Your Majesty, there are more than enough dragons to fight," said the Duke of Operations.

"In fact, our data show that the rate of dragon appearances has been increasing rather dramatically."

"Then why are we not raking it in?" asked the King. "Aren't our prices high enough?"

The Duke of Marketing cleared his throat. "Ahem. I believe that's part of the problem, Sire. Our prices may be too high. I'm sure it's only temporary, but it seems we've been losing a lot of citizens lately."

The King was stunned. "Losing citizens?! Have the dragons been eating our people? You know I won't stand for that!"

"Only a few have actually been eaten—"

"A few! How would you like it if *you* were one of the few?"

"But, Your Majesty," said the Duke of Operations, "we're doing the best we can! It's just that we're overwhelmed!"

"Then train more knights!" said the King. "Make more Magic Arrows!"

"Your Majesty, please!" said the Duke of Accounting. "Remember, the treasure chest is nearly empty!"

"Very well," said the King, "You have my permission to raise prices still further."

"As I was trying to explain, Your Majesty, our prices are already part of the problem," said the Duke of Marketing. "We are losing citizens not just because a few are being eaten, but because many others are leaving Lamron."

"What!? You mean to say our loyal Lamronians are leaving?"

"Sad but true, Sire. They are loyal no longer. They're bugging out. Hitting the highway."

"But why?"

The Duke of Market Research stepped forward. "Our surveys tell us that they're shopping around, Sire. They want faster service and lower prices—and they're willing to switch kingdoms to get them."

"But don't they know we're the best castle in the whole, wide magical world?" asked the King.

"Your Majesty," said the Duke of Marketing, "after our patent on Magic Arrows ran out, lots of brave young adventurers entered the dragon-fighting industry and they've established territories and built new castles."

"But not long ago, you assured me that these upstart castles were no threat to us!" said the King. "You assured me that we were still the best castle in the land!"

"Well, I'm afraid I didn't count on how fast the other castles would improve," said the duke. "We're still good, but they keep getting better!"

The King gave his dukes a dirty look and paced silently in front of them. Finally, he dismissed them, called for his carriage, and took a long ride into the countryside. Often, he stopped and talked to the Lamronians. And, wow, did they give the King an earful.

When the King got back, he said to the chief page, "Summon the trumpeters! We must have a meeting in the courtyard for all who work in the castle!"

Now, in those days, there were some rather strange things about working in Lamron Castle—strange yet so familiar that neither Art nor any of the other workers were alarmed by them.

For instance, there were no natural colors inside the castle walls. Everything and everybody in the castle was some shade of gray. No reds, no greens, no browns, no blues. It was all very gray in the castle.

Except on Monday mornings. The workers of the castle would come in looking like themselves. For a few hours, they would retain their natural colors. Then they turned gray like everything else. Didn't matter if you wore purple shoes and a yellow shirt, everything would be gray by noon.

Adding to the grayness was the fog. Every tower, every passageway, every room and chamber of the castle had a dark, misty fog drifting about it. No one knew from where it came, but the fog arrived at first light and never lifted until everyone went home. And somehow, when things were not going well, the fog seemed all the more dense.

The fog was so thick that it was impossible within the castle walls to do anything quickly. You couldn't even think quickly. When someone tried to get a job done fast, it was like trying to run through glue. Eventually, the poor person just gave up and went along at the speed the fog would allow.

These strange occurrences had been happening for so long that nobody thought much about them. They had ceased to be strange and instead had become normal.

Which is not to say that the people in the castle liked working in these conditions. Everybody just assumed that nothing could be done about them.

Despite the usual fog, everyone gathered in the court-yard of the castle, where the King made a stirring speech.

"Castle Lamron is good!" cried the King. "But we've got to get better!"

That was the King's keynote: We're good, but we've got to get better!"

And, great leader that he was, the King got everyone excited about this.

Things were going to be different!

Things were going to change!

At the end, they all sang a song and applauded one another wildly and went back to work. Something was in the air. They could sort of hear it. It was kind of a buzzing sound.

And even through the fog, they could almost see this energy. It was like lightning. And the lightning seemed to surround each person and make each one lively and energized. They were all charged up.

Even more amazing, the lightning had color—or rather it had hues of many colors. And the light of this lightning cut through the fog, making everyone brighter and able to see more clearly. With the light-ning around them, the castle workers' faces, hands, and clothes were less gray and more natural.

For the rest of the day, everyone in the castle worked with a fresh spirit and purpose. At the end of the day, they all went home, and when they came in the next morning, a lot of people still had that buzz, that flickering lightning about them. But many, just overnight, had lost it.

By the end of the second day, even those who still carried the lightning with them were less charged. And the third day, what lightning remained was even less. And so on until the lightning was gone and everything was gray and dull and slow again.

They did not yet have such things as batteries in this magic land, but that was what it was like after the King's speech: like charged-up batteries slowly discharging, going dead.

Every day the King watched for change within the castle. Surely after his stirring speech, the King thought, everybody would be motivated and performance would improve. But nothing got much better. The dragons kept coming, the castle's costs kept rising, and the citizens kept leaving.

So the King called in the dukes and said, "Look, we absolutely must improve or we've had it! What do I have to do, give a speech every day? Believe me, I'd do it, but we'd never get any work done! You dukes had better make things better or heads are going to roll!"

Not wanting heads to roll (especially not their own),

the dukes hurried high and low about the castle holding meetings with one another.

"The King is serious!" exclaimed the Duke of Operations. "This is not just another of His Majesty's pet projects! We really have to improve! But how? What shall we do?"

"I know!" said the Duke of Marketing, snapping his fingers. "Quick, we need an improvement program!"

"No, better yet, we need a *quick* improvement program!" said the Duke of Accounting.

"Great idea!" said the Duke of Operations. "I'll send a memo to the King so he knows we're doing something, and we'll get together again in a couple weeks to think up a catchy name!"

Then, with good intentions, off they rushed to other meetings and other dukely business.

Meanwhile, there were many besides the King who sensed how important it was for the castle to do a better job—and soon. They had only to look out the windows to see the dragons in the sky.

3

One day at lunch, Mac said to Art and Wendy, "You know, I think we've got to take this stuff seriously."

"What stuff?" asked Art.

"This stuff about doing better," said Mac. "Every time I look out the window of the Tower, I see more dragons, more castles crowding our territory, and more people like us hitting the highway."

"Yeah, well, whose fault is that?" asked Art. And he started blaming everyone: the knights, the King, the dukes, the Boss of Tower Two, the citizens, the other castles, his kids—

"Why are you blaming your kids?" asked Wendy.

"If it weren't for my kids," said Art, "I could quit and get out of this dingy gray castle and go down by the lake and carve ducks."

"You know what your problem is? You're just plain bored," said Wendy. "And you'd be just as bored carving ducks after a couple of years as you are here."

Art didn't say anything, which meant that she was probably right.

"Look, it's easy to blame everybody else. But that's not going to keep the dragons away," said Mac. "And even if you don't like your job, you do like where you're living, don't you? I mean, this is our home. I, for one, would like to keep living here. But without the castle, we're going to be on the highway with everyone else. Art won't even have anyone around to buy his ducks."

"Well, I agree," said Wendy. "But what can we do about it?"

"I think we can all try harder," said Mac.

"All right, I guess I could try a little harder," said Wendy. "What about you, Art?"

"Okay, okay," said Art. "Count me in."

The three of them shook hands on their agreement. And though they hardly noticed it, there was a tiny flicker of lightning between them when their hands met. It sounded a lot like the buzzing after the King's speech, only stronger. It sounded like . . .

Zapp!

For the next few days, try harder they did. Then, about the middle of the week, Mac asked them at lunch, "Well, how are you two doing? Are you still trying harder?"

"Sure," said Art.

"You bet," said Wendy.

"Me, too," said Mac.

They lifted their sandwiches in unison and ate lunch in silence for a minute.

Then Art said, "Hey, Mac, I've got a question."

"What's that?"

"I'm not sure I get it."

"Get what?"

"I've been working my behind off," said Art, "just like we three agreed. But what exactly are we trying harder to do?"

"Oh," said Mac. "Well, that's obvious, Art. We're trying to get more done."

"That's right," said Wendy. "To do better, you've got to get more done."

Art nodded. "Great. Get more done. Okay, now I understand."

A few more days went by and Mac asked them again, "How's it going with you two? Are you getting more done?"

"Yeah," said Art, "I'm getting tons more done."

"How about you, Wendy?"

"Yeah, I think so. At least I'm trying."

"Good, keep trying," said Mac. "If you keep working harder like Art and me, you'll get more done eventually."

"Yeah, like I did yesterday," said Art. "Yesterday I got a lot done."

"Did you? That's good," said Mac.

"Yeah, yesterday I spent hours cleaning my workbench and I polished it over and over until I could see myself in it," said Art. "And then I sharpened up all my tools until they were like razors."

"Terrific," said Mac.

"Yeah, by then I was really moving," said Art, "so I

went around and sharpened everybody else's tools, too."

"Fine," said Mac, "but how many arrow shafts did you turn out?"

"Oh, I didn't make any arrow shafts," said Art. "I was too busy getting all that other stuff done."

"Art! When we talk about working harder and getting more done, we don't mean more tools sharpened or workbenches polished!" said Mac. "We mean *get more arrows done!*"

"How am I going to do that? I only make the shafts," said Art.

"You've got to turn out more shafts, and I've got to make more heads, and Wendy has to do more wand-waving. Then, as a result, there will be more arrows finished," Mac patiently explained.

Now, it may appear that Art Halegiver was a bit dense. In fact, Art was fairly smart. But after years of working in the fog and doing the same thing over and over again the same way every day, his brain had become somewhat stupefied. He had stopped thinking as well as he once had. And, as one result, he had lost sight of the big picture.

"Art, you've got to remember what's important," said Wendy.

"You're telling me that sharp tools are not important?" asked Art.

"Sharp tools are important," said Mac, "but only if in the end they help you turn out more shafts. That's the really important thing: for the whole Tower to make more Magic Arrows. If you spend more time sharpening tools than making arrow shafts, then something is wrong."

"Okay, so you want me to make more arrow shafts," said Art, "so that the whole Tower can make more Magic Arrows. That's what's really important?"

"Well, yeah," said Mac. "At least I can't think of anything more important. Can you, Wendy?"

"No, that's what the Boss always seems to be harping about, more Magic Arrows. So you've got to do your part, Art, and make more shafts."

"Okay," said Art, "I'll do my best. More shafts are on the way."

Again, they shook hands on their agreement to try harder.

And again there was a small flash of lightning between them and a tiny sound—*Zapp!*—both of which went unnoticed in the thick fog.

When Art got back to his worktable in the Shaftshop, he shook his head, as if shaking away cobwebs inside, and laughed at himself. The past few days, he'd been doing all this extra work and thinking, What good is this going to do?

Now his brain began to regain some of its old sharpness and he concluded this:

If some action truly helped him turn out more arrow shafts by the end of the day, then it was productive. If it didn't or if it hurt his output, then it was not productive. It was that simple.

So he made a note of this and tacked it to the wall, which was just his way of reminding himself of these things as he worked.

FROM THE WORKBENCH OF: **ART HALEGIVER**

Tower Two Lamron Castle

Reminder to Me: Figure Out What's Important! (And What's Not)

Most important (for the whole Tower): More Magic Arrows!

For my job: More Arrow Shafts!

A few days later, over lunch, Mac asked the same question as before, only he tried to be more specific. "How are you two doing? Are you getting more done? Are we finishing more arrows?"

Wendy looked the other way, and Art took a bite of a banana so he wouldn't have to talk.

"What's the matter?" asked Mac. "You're both trying harder and getting more done, aren't you?"

They both nodded.

"Then we must be turning out more arrows, right?"

Art shrugged his shoulders. "I don't know; I guess so."

"What's the matter?" asked Mac. "Can't you tell?"

"How should I know how much I'm getting done?" asked Art.

"He's right," said Wendy. "That's been my problem, too. Sometimes it feels like I'm getting more done. But I don't really know."

Mac hung his head for a moment. "The truth is, I've been having the same trouble. Even when it seems like I'm having an extra-good day, I'm never sure."

"I know," said Wendy, "why don't we go talk to the Boss and find out how we're doing?"

"What?!" said Art. "Are you crazy?"

"What's wrong with talking to the Boss?"

"Gee, I don't know," Art said uncertainly, "but it just doesn't seem like a good idea. I mean, what if the Boss thinks we're just trying to get brownie points?"

"So what?"

"Or worse, what if everyone else in Tower Two

thinks we're going for brownie points?" asked Mac.

"Oh, come on, you guys, relax!" said Wendy. "We just need to get some information!"

So they went to see the Boss.

"What can I do for you?" asked the Boss of Tower Two as they walked into her office.

"We're trying to figure out how well we're doing," said Wendy.

"Right, so that we can improve," said Art.

The Boss looked at them as if they were weird. "Are you three going for brownie points or what?"

"No!" said Mac. "We're just trying to do our bit to make sure the castle isn't overrun by all the dragons out there."

The Boss considered this. "So you're sincere."

"Yes," said Wendy, "and we wanted to ask you for some numbers—"

"Numbers? What kind of numbers?" the Boss asked suspiciously.

"Numbers that would tell us how well we're doing," said Art. "You know, like how many arrow shafts am I turning out each day? And how many arrowheads is Mac making? And how many finished Magic Arrows are getting to the knights?"

"Oh, those kinds of numbers," said the Boss. She got up from her chair and began herding them toward the door. "Well, you don't need to worry yourselves about numbers. Believe me, if you start slipping, I'll be the first to let you know."

"But that's not the point," argued Art. "We want to

set a standard for ourselves so that we see if we're improving."

"I'm sure you do," said the Boss, "but unfortunately I can't share numbers with you."

"Why not?"

"It's against castle policy."

"Since when?"

"Since forever."

"But why?"

"Well . . . think about it," said the Boss. "What if one of the other castles got hold of our numbers?"

"But we won't tell anybody," said Wendy.

"Uh-huh. Listen, you three just keep working real hard," said the Boss, "and let me and the dukes worry about how we're doing."

And with that she nudged them out her door.

As they made their way through the fog, Wendy grumbled to the others, "How come the Boss, the dukes, and the King can know how we're doing, but they won't tell us?"

"You know what it's like?" asked Art. "It's like playing ball here in the castle."

Every other Tuesday, the castle employees played ball down in the south courtyard, where there was a nice ball field and an expensive scoreboard, which magically kept the numbers on both teams.

There was only one problem: The fog in the castle was so thick that none of the players could ever read what the scoreboard said. Nobody ever knew the score—until the end of the game, when someone got a ladder and a lantern and put his or her face up next to the numbers.

This lack of information made the games rather perplexing and at the same time rather dull, because no one ever knew who was ahead and who was behind. Which was why they only played every few weeks, even though everybody loved to play ball; without knowing the score, what was the point?

"Well, then," said Mac, "why don't we three do what I suggested to all the castle ball players a long time ago—even though no one ever took my advice."

"What's that?" asked Wendy.

"If we can't see the big scoreboard, then let's not rely on it," said Mac. "Let's keep our own score. Then we'll know if this extra effort we're making is paying off or not."

"How are we going to do that?"

"We have to measure what we do," said Mac, "on our own."

They all looked at one another and nodded together.

"Fine, let's do it," said Art.

4

And so they agreed to do their own measurements—easy, simple measurements. After all, as Wendy pointed out, if they kept elaborate measurements, they'd have that much less time to make Magic Arrows, which was the important thing.

So they just kept pads and pens next to where they were working, and when they finished something, they made a note of it. Art simply made hash marks for the arrow shafts he finished, like this ...

$$\cancel{||||} \quad \cancel{||||} \quad \cancel{||||}$$
$$\cancel{||||} \quad \cancel{||||}$$

It was not a big deal. But the effect was unexpectedly large.

A few days after they started keeping count, Art

started hearing a funny sound. It was sort of like that buzzing sound after the King's big speech, but it was stronger.

The sound came when he looked at the pad where he kept count of his arrow shafts and realized how much he had got done. Of course, it was a sound that had been there for some time, but until now had not been loud enough for him to hear:

Zapp!

And he felt around him a sort of electricity. It was a power that comes from awareness combined with accomplishment. Until now, about the only time he had felt this was on the ball field. He did not believe it at first, but to his amazement, he was now feeling it at work—in a job he long had not liked.

Why?

Well, as Art Halegiver thought about it, when he took the initiative and started keeping his own measurements of his work, he put himself in control. Though he had not meant to, he had started to empower himself.

And as that happened, he began to feel better. Even his work area seemed brighter, the fog less dense.

When he looked down at his hands and his body, it seemed there was a light around them that was not quite visible, yet it was there.

The three of them went to lunch at the end of the week, and as soon as Art looked at his friends, he said, "I see it's happening to you, too."

"Yeah, probably some side effect of the wizards doing

some magical experiments down in the R&D Dungeon," suggested Mac.

"No, I think it's us," said Wendy. "It's something we are doing to ourselves."

"Doing to ourselves?" asked Mac. "What could we possibly be doing to ourselves?"

"We're taking charge is what we're doing," said Wendy.

"We're not in charge of anything," Mac argued.

"Yes, we are," said Art. "We're in charge of our own work."

"That's right," said Wendy. "We took charge when we agreed among the three of us."

"Then maybe we should stop," said Mac. "I know I'm the one who got us started on this, but I don't know what we're getting into."

"Stop?!" said Art. "I don't want to stop now. This is the first time in years I've felt halfway good about my job!"

"Besides, what are we doing that's bad?" Wendy asked. "All we did was agree that we'd try to do better because the dragons are winning, we started to figure out what's important, and now we're keeping track of how well we're doing. What's wrong with any of those?"

"Nothing," Mac admitted. "I just have this strange feeling."

In fact, it took Mac a while to figure out what the feeling was when he heard the sound of Zapp! and got that energy around him. It took him a while because he had not felt this feeling in some time. But after a while he put a name to it.

It was pride.

At one of their lunches some weeks later, the three of them tried to put into words what Zapp! was and what it was like to be Zapped. Art wrote these words down.

FROM THE WORKBENCH OF: **ART HALEGIVER**

Tower Two Lamron Castle

Zapp! is the energizing feeling that comes with greater knowledge, greater skill, and greater control.

When you have been Zapped you feel like . . .
- **You are in charge of your own work.**
- **Your job belongs to you.**
- **You are responsible.**
- **You are capable of improving.**
- **You know what's important, what's going on.**
- **You have pride in what you do.**

The charge from Zapp! is very positive.

Meanwhile, Art noticed that just by keeping count he often got a little bit more done with little or no extra effort. Maybe it was just human nature; now that he knew the score, he just naturally wanted to make it go higher. But often, by studying the numbers, he could see better what was happening to slow him down and screw him up.

Whatever the reason, the count of arrow shafts he made did go higher. And when the score went higher, Art kept feeling better and better.

Zapp!

Every few days, Art would ask the others, "How many did you do?"

"I did twenty-one yesterday."

"I finished twenty-six, which is better than the day before."

And so on and so on.

They soon figured out that there was no comparison between a "twenty-one" by Mac and a "thirty-two" by Art and a "twenty-six" by Wendy, because it took different amounts of time and effort to do their different jobs. It was apples to oranges to compare one person's numbers with another's.

The numbers in themselves meant nothing. What created the Zapp! was beating the numbers.

Of course, measurement was nothing new to Tower Two.

The Boss kept all kinds of numbers and measures. Almost every day, a disembodied eye would float through the Tower counting and recording everything it saw.

The wizards had developed these floating eyes years ago as a way of gathering information, but they had not thought to include a mouth with the eye so that the information could be shared. Not even the Boss had access to everything the eyes picked up.

The floating eyes gave all the arrow-makers the willies. Everybody hated them. They were not enZapping at all. More the opposite. The fog and darkness were always much thicker and deeper after the eyes drifted through.

But measuring your own performance, as Art and the others discovered, was quite different. It was a good Zapp! to know how you were really doing.

Over time, though, they found that their output tended to level off and average out.

"How many did you get done today?"

"About the same as yesterday."

"I did about average for me."

Even knowing the score, they found that the game was becoming a bit dull, the Zapps were becoming fewer.

"You know what we need?" said Art. "We need something to shoot for. We need a goal."

"All right," said Wendy, "but what should the goal be?"

"I don't know," said Art. "Let's just each pick our own goal and go for it."

"Wait a minute," Mac said. "How do we know that the goal we each pick is really going to make a difference if we reach it? If we're going to set a goal for ourselves and bust our tails to reach it, then there ought to be some kind of meaning to it."

"Maybe we should talk to the Boss," suggested Wendy.

"Why do you always want to talk to the Boss?!" asked Mac. "The last time we talked to her, she was no help at all!"

"Because it's a boss's job to know what's what," said Wendy. "She is supposed to know what we're all trying to accomplish, so she should be the one to help us set good goals."

Grumbling, Mac reluctantly agreed, and later that day they went once again to see the Boss.

"What's up?" asked the Boss.

"Well," said Wendy, "we've been trying to improve our work, and we thought that it would help us to have a goal in mind."

"A goal for yourselves? You mean something to shoot for?" asked the Boss.

"Right, a meaningful goal," said Art. "Something that when we reach it will really have an impact and make a difference."

"Good idea!" said the Boss. "Hmmm ... Let me think for a minute." She put a hand on her chin for a few seconds, then got a big smile, stood up, and patted them each on the shoulder. "Here's a goal for you: Keep doing more! That's your goal. Just keep doing more! If you keep doing more, you'll never run out of things to do!"

The three arrow-makers held their tongues until they were out of the Boss's office, then Art and Mac let Wendy have it.

"Gee, that was terrific, Wendy," Mac said sarcastically. "That was really helpful!"

"Yeah, Wendy. 'Just keep doing more!' she says. What a great goal!" said Art. "That's like being in the middle of the ocean and the boat captain keeps yelling, 'Paddle faster!' Never mind where we're going! Never mind if we're ever going to reach land!"

"If all she's ever going to want is more, More, MORE, why are we even trying?" asked Mac.

"Okay, I agree! She's not the greatest boss in the world!" said Wendy. "But she's the only boss we've got and we have to deal with her."

They walked a way in the fog of Tower Two. Then Art asked, "So what should we do now?"

"Let's go back to your idea. Let's just pick our own individual goals and let it go at that," said Mac.

"Yeah, I guess so," said Art. "Wendy, what do you think?"

But Wendy was staring into space.

"Wendy?"

She came back to reality. "Sorry. I was thinking."

"About what?"

"I was thinking about who else we could ask to find out

what's really important and what kind of goal we should shoot for. And I thought maybe we should talk to the King."

Indeed, the castle had an open-door policy. Though the King was the King, anyone could talk to him. One had only to go to the Throne Room.

"Yeah," said Mac, "but if we do that, we're liable to make the Boss mad because we'll be going over her head."

"Right, and there's another problem," said Wendy. "The King is concerned about the whole castle. He's not going to know what we should be doing down here in Tower Two. But then I remembered something my dad always said before he moved away: The customer is the real king, because the customer is always right."

"So?" asked Mac.

"So why don't we talk to customers and find out what they think? Maybe we'll find out enough information to set our own goals."

This was a brilliant idea, both Mac and Art thought. The very next day, the three of them went into town for lunch, ate quickly, and then spent the rest of the time going door to door asking the citizens questions like "How many Magic Arrows do you think Tower Two ought to produce?"

Door after door, they got a lot of strange looks. They even got a few doors slammed in their faces. What they didn't get was information that would let them set goals for themselves.

"I don't care one rat's tail how many arrows Tower Two produces!" said one cranky old man. "I just want the knights to show up and the dragons to go away when

I get on the horn!"

A bit disappointed, Wendy, Mac, and Art went back to work.

"Well, Wendy, you're two for two," Mac chided.

"What are you blaming me for? I don't hear you guys coming up with ideas that are any better."

"Obviously, those people were not the right customers to talk to," Art said in her defense, "or they would have had an opinion about what we do."

"What do you mean they're not the right ones to talk to?" said Mac. "Who do you think pays the bills?"

Later that same day, however, the three of them were called to the Boss's office. With the Boss was a towering, handsome man in armor.

"This is Sir Fred, the Captain of the King's Knights," said the Boss. "He wants to know if the three of you were in town at lunch today."

"Why, yes, we were," said Mac.

"Then you three must have been the ones knocking on the doors of the townspeople," said Sir Fred.

"It's true, we were," said Wendy. "Something wrong with that?"

"You shouldn't be bothering our customers," said Sir Fred.

"We were just trying to get a better idea of how many arrows we should be making," said Art. "What's wrong with that?"

"If you want to know that, you should have talked to me!" said Sir Fred. "After all, it's the knights who depend on your arrows."

"Aha!" said Art. "So you and the knights are our customers!"

"Well … true, I guess you could put it that way."

"Good," said Wendy. "Then maybe you can help us. We want a goal to reach—a meaningful goal, one that would count for something in the fight against the dragons."

"I thought we agreed you were just going to try to do more," said the Boss.

"Well, we are trying to do more," said Art.

"But as a goal, 'doing more' is too vague," said Mac. "We need something specific."

"Okay," said the Boss, and she turned to Sir Fred. "I know you and the knights are always complaining that you don't have enough Magic Arrows. So here's a golden opportunity. How many Magic Arrows do you think these people should try to produce?"

"Hmmm," said Sir Fred. "I'm not sure. But I do know that we never have enough."

"Couldn't you give us a number to try to reach?"

Just then, there was the sound of horns from the countryside and trumpets blared from the Main Gate, calling the knights to their saddles.

"Uh-oh," said Sir Fred, "that's a four-dragon alarm. I've gotta run. Look, just make double the number of arrows you make now. I'm sure that'll be enough."

And Sir Fred ran off to fight dragons.

"There," the Boss said to the three. "How's that for a goal?"

When they got outside, Art said, "Well, at least we found out who our real customers are."

Wendy said, "But I can't believe it! Double?!"

"You heard it," said Mac. "Make *double* the number of arrows we're making now."

"He really said 'double,' didn't he?" said Art.

"That jerk said '*double'!*" said Mac. "Well, that'll teach us to go ask dumb questions. We should have just picked numbers on our own."

"But, Mac, we have to pick numbers that mean something or we're just playing games," argued Wendy. "You know, I personally think we did the right thing, even if other people gave us an answer we didn't want to hear."

"But it's an impossible goal," said Mac. "We'll never be able to do it."

"Wait," said Art, "how do you know it's impossible? And what if the knights really do need double the number of Magic Arrows we're putting out? Shouldn't we at least try to make that many for them?"

"You're nuts!" said Mac. "We'll never do double what we're doing now!"

"Listen, I'm not going to kill myself over it," said Wendy. "But I go along with Art. We should at least try."

"I'm telling you, it's impossible."

"Maybe not," said Art. "You know what we need? We need one of those, you know, what-do-you-call-its— one of those ideas that geniuses think up that lets you do something that you could never do before."

"You mean a breakthrough?" asked Wendy.

"That's it! That's it!" said Art. "We need a break-through!"

Mac rolled his eyes. "Well, I hate to tell you this, Artie, but breakthroughs don't come easy."

"We could still try to think one up, couldn't we?"

"Yeah. You go right ahead," said Mac as he wandered off into the fog. "As for me, I'm going back to doing things the way I've always done them."

The next time they got together, Art had a strange smile on his face.

"What are you grinning about?" Mac asked.

"You know how we were talking about break-throughs?"

"So?"

"Well, I came up with one," said Art.

"You did? What is it?" asked Wendy.

Art leaned forward. "It's a secret!"

"You can tell us," said Wendy. "We're all friends. We've been working together for years."

"No, I'm not telling anybody what it is. I'm just going to do it on my own," said Art. "But I can tell you this: With my idea, we'll be turning out twice as many arrows. In fact, I'm surprised nobody has thought of this before."

A day later, everyone knew about Art Halegiver's brilliant breakthrough.

5

The next afternoon, there was a big ruckus in Tower Two when the Boss came storming through.

"Who made the shafts for these arrows?" she demanded.

Art Halegiver took one look and proudly recognized his own work. Smile on his face, he said, "I did!"

"This isn't an arrow!" yelled the Boss, holding a sample in the air. "This is a dart!"

Indeed, the tiny arrow she held was half the length of the typical Tower Two arrow.

"But that's my big breakthrough!" said Art.

"What breakthrough? What are you talking about?"

"Sir Fred said we had to double our output. So I cut all my arrow shafts in half and made twice as many!" said Art. "Pretty smart, huh?"

The Boss glared at him. "Sir Fred has just informed me that these puny little arrows do not fit their bows! They can't pull the strings back because the arrows aren't long enough!"

"Oh," said Art. He began to blush with embarrassment. "I didn't think of that."

"All your shafts from yesterday are going to have to be scrapped," said the Boss. Then she quietly added, "Look, I know you and your friends are trying. But the next time you come up with a breakthrough, will you please tell me about it first?"

"Sure," said Art. "Sorry."

Word of Art's failed breakthrough spread quickly through the ranks of the arrow-makers. Art became the target of not a few jokes.

Over lunch, as Mac and Wendy tried to console him, Art said, "You know, the worst part wasn't that the Boss yelled at me. The worst part was that I was actually having a good time at work—for the first time in years. Maybe the first time ever."

"You were?" asked Wendy. "I thought you were always bored."

"I was, until we started seeing the big picture and keeping track of what we were doing and figuring out how we could do better," said Art. "Then I came up with my idea, and that really was fun, because it was *my* idea and I was making it happen."

"Too bad it didn't work," said Mac.

"Well, maybe you'll come up with another idea," said Wendy. "And maybe that idea will be better."

A few weeks went by. Mac had given up asking everyone how well they were doing. In fact, Mac considered the whole "try harder" campaign to be all but a complete failure.

So Mac was surprised when Art volunteered the information over lunch one day that he was now turning out more than thirty arrow shafts a day, five better than his previous average.

"Good for you," said Mac.

A few more weeks went by. Art announced he was now up to thirty-three arrow shafts a day.

Then it was thirty-eight shafts a day.

A little while later it was forty-two.

A couple of weeks after that it was forty-six.

And shortly after that it was fifty-one.

"Wow," said Wendy. "You've done it! You've doubled your output!"

"You're not making this up, are you?" asked Mac. "You're really doing twice what you used to do?"

"Yeah," said Art. "I really am. My numbers don't lie."

"You must be killing yourself down there," said Mac. "You must be dead tired by the time you get home at night."

"No," said Art. "To tell you the truth, I feel pretty good. I mean, I'm tired, but I'm not working much harder than before. And, I don't know what it is, but I feel better than ever."

"Then how are you doing it?" asked Mac.

Art leaned in close to him and tapped his forefinger on the side of his skull. "Brainpower, buddy boy, brainpower!"

That afternoon, Mac found an excuse to go down to

the Shaftshop and check out Art Halegiver's work area. He was surprised to see that, at first glance, there was nothing dramatically different about Art's work area from the way it had always looked—except that there was a lot less fog than in most of the Tower's work areas and that Art himself seemed to be surrounded by a bright field of lightninglike energy. But so what?

"Okay, I want to know how you're really doing it," Mac said to Art.

"I told you, I'm using—"

"Yeah, yeah, yeah," said Mac. "Now level with me, what are you actually doing that's let you get so good?"

"Well," said Art, "it came to me one morning when I woke up. My breakthrough was on the right track. It was just the wrong approach."

"How do you mean?" asked Mac.

"Here, take a look," said Art. "I wrote it down."

FROM THE WORKBENCH OF: **ART HALEGIVER**

Tower Two Lamron Castle

CUT THE PROCESS, NOT THE ARROWS!

"But how can you cut the process?" Mac asked.

"One little idea at a time," said Art.

Then he showed Mac all the many little ways he had thought up to cut the work process.

Like he'd reorganized all his tools so that he knew where they were by touch and he didn't have to spend an extra few seconds looking for them.

And he'd taken a section out of his worktable and moved everything closer together. That meant he only had to take one step rather than two or three.

Then he got a stool with wheels on the legs so that if he got tired near the end of the day, he could wheel himself back and forth and not have to slow down.

"You and Wendy got down on me when I spent all that time sharpening my tools," said Art, "but I found that sharp tools give me an extra four or five shafts a day because they cut faster and I don't make as many mistakes."

That was another thing: He worked at eliminating mistakes. Of course, being human, he made plenty of them. But, being human, he also had a mind that allowed him to set up little systems that would prevent him from doing something dumb in a thoughtless moment.

"But the biggest little improvement," said Art, "is this."

He held up a homemade-looking gadget that did not seem at all impressive—until he proceeded to demonstrate.

The gadget was a special jig he'd rigged that would let

him cut five shafts at a time, and then it would hold them in place while he cut slots for the feathers and notches for the arrowheads.

This saved him only about an hour out of every day, but that meant he had an extra hour to turn more shafts on his lathe. So the combination of saved time and extra time meant he had about a 25 percent jump—enough in combination with all the other little improvements to add up to a big improvement.

"But anybody could have done what you did!" said Mac.

"But *any*body didn't," said Art. "*I* did."

Mac went away jealous. The next day, however, he started trying the same kinds of things in the Arrowhead Area.

Soon, he was the one at lunch bragging about his numbers: "Did thirty-two yesterday." And, "Up to thirty-four now." And, "Big day today, I could pass forty arrowheads."

By and by, he was turning out fifty arrowheads and started aiming at sixty. It was only a matter of time, he felt, before he, too, would double his output.

Now, about this time, the Boss was absent one day from Tower Two. She along with all the bosses of all the towers in the castle had been called to a big meeting. Everybody who was the boss of anybody was there. And it was at this big meeting that the dukes announced "the QIP."

"QIP," of course, stood for "Quick Improvement Program." And it was at this meeting that dukes stood up one by one and said in effect the same thing, which was: "Quick! We need improvement!"

Last to speak was the Duke of Operations, who said, "We expect a ten percent improvement from everybody in the castle by the next Dragon Moon!"

When she heard this, the Boss of Tower Two started having an anxiety attack. Because what the dukes did not explain was how she and the other bosses were supposed to achieve that 10 percent improvement. For motivation, the dukes passed out calendars with the date of the Dragon Moon circled.

The Dragon Moon was the castle's busy season, a time when dragon sightings often doubled or tripled—and the next one was not far off.

You see, like almost everyone else in the castle, the Boss of Tower Two had been doing her job the same way for so long that she didn't know how to change. And of course it is impossible to improve without some kind of change taking place. So the Boss was in a pickle.

High and low through Tower Two went the Boss, saying to each arrow-maker, "Let's go! I need ten percent more from each of you!"

But when she got to Mac, he looked her straight in the eye and said, "I've already given you an eighty percent improvement."

"Go on," said the Boss.

"It's a fact. I know because I've been keeping my own numbers."

The Boss was shocked and amazed. She suspected Mac of making this up. "Well, I'll have to check my records and see if this is true."

This she did, and sure enough, according to data collected by the floating eyes, Mac was right. She also noticed that another arrow-maker, one Art Halegiver, had achieved a 100 percent improvement in recent moons.

The next day the Boss saw Mac and Art having lunch with Wendy in the courtyard, and figuring (correctly) that she would need all the allies she could get before the next Dragon Moon, she hurried over.

"Art, Mac! Congratulations to both of you! You two are doing exceptionally well. Mac, you are the top head-shaper of Tower Two. And Art, you are not only the top shaft-turner of Tower Two, but of the entire castle."

"What did I tell you," said Mac.

"Well, keep up the good work," said the Boss and added, looking at Wendy, "If the rest of the arrow-makers would do as well as you two, maybe we'd finally be able to get more Magic Arrows to the knights."

"What do you mean?" asked Art. "Haven't we been delivering more arrows to the knights?"

"Well, in a word," said the Boss, "no."

"How can that be?" asked Art. "I've doubled my output and Mac has nearly doubled his! There ought to be some kind of increase in the finished arrows, shouldn't there?"

"No, not according to my reports," said the Boss.

"We're still making the same number of Magic Arrows as always."

After the Boss left, both Mac and Art turned to Wendy.

"Why are you looking at me like that?" she asked.

"Because wand-waving is the last step of arrow-making," said Art, "and it's obvious that you wand-wavers are not doing your bit. Otherwise, with all the added output that Mac and I are turning out, there would be a huge rise in the number of finished arrows. Am I right or what?"

"Look, I've been trying!" she said. "Maybe if you told me the kinds of things you both are doing I could do better."

So they let Wendy in on their "little" secret and she, too, began looking for small ways to improve.

FROM THE WORKBENCH OF: **ART HALEGIVER**

Tower Two Lamron Castle

- **Big "Little" Secrets: Little gains can add up in time to a big improvement.**

- **Little goals mark the road to bigger goals.**

- **Making a lot of little improvements can be more effective than chasing after a big breakthrough.**

So day by day, Wendy looked for ways to save a step here and prevent a mistake there. And she found them.

Before long, she was finishing her wand-waving a little bit earlier every day. After a while, she found that by early afternoon, she was done; there were no more arrows ready for her to wave her wand at.

This became boring. So she began to help out the other wand-wavers. And in a matter of weeks, all of the wand-wavers at the top of Tower Two were done by mid-afternoon—no more arrows to work on until the following morning.

When Art Halegiver heard about this, he said, "Wow! We must be really turning out the arrows now!"

The next time Art saw the Boss, he said, "Hey, Boss, how about that big increase in finished arrows?"

"What big increase?" asked the Boss.

"Check the numbers! We must be finishing at least twice the Magic Arrows we used to!"

So the Boss checked the latest report and said to Art, "No, sorry, but we're still putting out about the same number of arrows as always."

"What? That's impossible. There has to have been an increase!"

"Well, I'm not supposed to show you the numbers," said the Boss, "but since you're one of my best arrow-makers, take a look for yourself."

Indeed, Art saw that for many moons, the average daily output of finished Magic Arrows had stayed pretty much the same. He went to his friends to complain.

"I just don't get it. Mac and I are turning out double

what we used to. Wendy is finishing her work faster. Why hasn't there been an improvement?"

The answer suddenly dawned on Wendy.

"We can't be finishing more arrows," she said, "because I'm not getting more arrows into the Magic Room. The arrows that I do get, I'm finishing faster because I'm now more efficient. But the total number has not increased, because we wand-wavers are still getting the same number of arrows as always."

"That's impossible!" said Art. "What about all the extra pieces Mac and I are making? Where are they all going?"

"Let's take a walk through the Tower and find out," said Mac.

They didn't have to go far. Just upstairs above the Shaftshop was the Feather Floor, where feathers were glued to the arrow shafts. As soon as Art opened the door, bundles and bundles of shafts spilled out and rolled down the stairs. There were hundreds of arrow shafts piled floor to ceiling, all waiting for the feather-gluers to stick the feathers on one end.

And upstairs from the Arrowhead Area was the Twine-Tying Room. Here, Mac, Art, and Wendy found buckets and buckets of arrowheads and bundles and bundles of feathered arrow shafts—all waiting for someone to tie the heads to the shafts with twine.

Meanwhile, what were the feather-gluers and the twine-tiers doing? They were working the same old way as always.

"What are we going to do?" asked Wendy. "We can't

make double the Magic Arrows that Sir Fred said he needed—we can't even reach that ten percent improvement that the Boss said she needed—without the feather-gluers and the twine-tiers!"

"I know!" said Art. "It doesn't make any difference if the three of us do twice as much if everyone else stays the same!"

"You're right," said Mac. "We've got to get all the functions in the Tower—the shaft-turners, the head-shapers, the feather-gluers, the twine-tiers, *and* the wand-wavers—to improve … or we're stuck."

"We've got to get them to help," said Art.

"But how?" asked Wendy. "How can we get everyone else to work with us? How do we get them involved? How can we persuade them to do the things they should be doing?"

Indeed, for all the years they'd been working at the castle, nothing had prepared them for this. They were used to coming to work, doing what the Boss told them to do, getting it done individually, and then going home at the end of the day.

But now, in order to save themselves and the castle and the whole land of Lamron, they had to change not only themselves, but other people, too.

They had to get everyone to work together. Like a team. They had no idea where to begin.

FROM THE WORKBENCH OF: **ART HALEGIVER**

Tower Two Lamron Castle

- **Every job has an effect on every other job ahead of it and behind it.**

- **An improvement by one person doesn't necessarily mean an improvement for the whole Tower.**

- **We need to think in terms of improving the whole Tower, not just one job function!**

- **To do this, we have to get all the arrow-makers involved.**

- **Individual success depends on gaining the support of others.**

6

"Well," said Mac. "I think I know what to do." He got a grim, determined look in his eye. "Don't worry, I'll take care of this right now."

And take care of it, he did.

Mac went up and down through Tower Two yelling, "What's wrong with you people? Don't you know the knights need more arrows? Get a move on! Let's go!"

By the end of the day, except for Art and Wendy, Mac had lost all his friends. And his enemies didn't like him any better either.

"Hey, Mac, who put you in charge? Who are you to tell us what to do?" both friends and enemies silently (and not so silently) asked. Everybody resented being told what to do by an equal.

It was soon clear that Mac's hard-line approach did not work. Everybody continued plodding along at the same old pace, doing their jobs the same way as always. If anything, they did less, because they were mad at Mac.

"They're just not as tough as I am," Mac grumbled. "Especially these younger arrow-makers. They just can't take it."

"Mac, you can't yell at people and expect them to support you," said Art.

"Why don't I give it a try?" said Wendy. "I think I know how to get the others to support us."

The next morning she came to work with bouquets of flowers, and she went around to everyone in the Tower and gave each person a flower. Then she sang a little song about what a wonderful world it was and what wonderful people they were.

Then she said sweetly, "Oh, please, please, please, help us make more arrows!"

The response to Wendy's approach was not much better. Most people just smiled and backed away, and when she'd gone, they turned to one another and went, "Yecht!" A few, usually in the middle of the song, ran for the nearest window and upchucked into the courtyard.

But in the end nobody did anything to help increase the number of Magic Arrows coming from Tower Two.

For a couple of days, Wendy didn't show up for lunch. Concerned, Mac and Art went to look for her. They searched Tower Two high and low and finally found her on the roof.

"How come you're hiding up here?" asked Mac.

"I'm not hiding," she said. "I'm just mad at everyone. They're all a bunch of jerks."

"Let me guess why," said Art. "You tried to reach out to people and nobody responded the way you thought they would."

"I was as nice as I could be!" Wendy sulked. "Why didn't they cooperate?"

"I guess because it just takes more than being nice—or being tough—to get people to do things," said Art.

"Then what's the answer?" asked Wendy.

"I don't know," said Art.

"I don't know either," said Mac as he looked over the wall. "But we'd better figure out something pretty quick, because—well, take a look for yourselves."

Just down the road, in plain view from the roof of the tower, was a dragon. A big dragon. It had just glided down from the sky.

"Wow," said Art. "I've never seen one this close."

"Sure is ugly," said Mac.

"How come the lookouts haven't spotted it?" said Wendy.

"I guess most of them are at lunch," said Art.

"Somebody had better warn that guy down there."

"What guy?"

"The guy who's about to become toast."

Indeed, there was a tall, thin, strangely dressed man walking along the road with his back to the dragon.

"Hey, buddy! Hey!" Mac yelled down to the man. "Look out behind you!"

Just then, the enormous dark shadow of the dragon fell over the man on the road. The man looked over his shoulder and suddenly understood what kind of trouble he was in. He started to run, but in one swipe, the dragon had the man in its talons.

Now, that would have been it for the poor guy, except for one thing: Dragons often like to play with their food. It can be several minutes, sometimes several hours, before a dragon gets around to eating its dinner. This undesirable character trait has actually saved many a Lamronian, giving the knights time to charge to the scene and shoot their arrows.

The dragon, as it heated up its fire breath, began to toss the helpless man into the air, juggling him from one clawed paw to the next, bouncing him off its tail and so on. This gave Art Halegiver time to run downstairs and grab some Magic Arrows and the bow occasionally used for quality-control testing.

He got back to the roof, drew an arrow, shot—and missed.

His second shot did better. He hit the dragon in the head, but the arrow bounced off.

Then, by luck, his third shot hit the dragon in the heart. The beast began to shrink. Smaller and smaller got the dragon, until it was so small that the man was bigger than the monster. The man broke free of its dragon's grasp, gave the beast a swift kick, and ran toward the castle. A few seconds later the dragon vanished completely in a brilliant burst of light.

Art, Mac, and Wendy ran to the Main Gate to greet the strangely dressed man, who came huffing and puffing over the drawbridge.

"Thanks, you saved my life," said the man.

"No problem," said Art. "Are you okay?"

"A few cuts and bruises, but I'll live," said the man. "Is there anything I can do to repay you?"

"Don't worry about it. I'm sure you'd have done the same for us."

"Well, if there is ever anything I can do to help you out ... " The man took a business card from his wallet and handed it to the three arrow-makers.

DAVID D. IGNATIUS
Zapp! Wizard
Spells of Empowerment For All

"Just call me Dave," said the man.

"You're a wizard?" asked Mac.

"That's right."

"You're dressed kind of strange for a wizard," said Mac. "Most wizards I know wear long robes and pointy hats."

Dave glanced down at his white shirt, business suit, and tie, then said, "I'm not like most wizards."

"I guess not," said Wendy. "I thought you wizards carried a spell or two with you to ward off dragon attacks."

"Well, I practice a different kind of magic," said Dave. "See, there are two kinds of magic. You've got your Technical Magic, like the kind that goes into your Magic Arrows. That kind of magic fights dragons, cures warts, and amuses small children. And then you've got Zapp! Magic, which is what gives people a special kind of power to be at their best. That's what my spells are all about."

"What exactly do your spells do?" asked Wendy.

"Depends on the spell," said Dave. "But most of my spells build a better workplace with less fog and more energy to get things done. Some of my spells help solve problems. Others let people support one another so that the whole group can reach its goals. Best of all, my spells help people enjoy their jobs more. Work is a big part of life, you know, and if we have to work for a living, why not get more out of it than just the gold we earn?"

"Yes, that's a very interesting attitude," said Wendy.

"Did you say something about your spells helping people to support one another?" asked Art.

"Yes, I did. Well, I'd love to talk about it, but I've got to get going," said Dave. "It's not a coincidence I'm here today. I'm on my way to see the King. Got an appointment. In fact, I'd better get to the Throne Room or I'll be late."

"Wait a minute. You know, there might be a way you can repay that favor you owe us," said Mac.

"How so?"

"I think we might be able to use some of your magic around here."

"Great! If the King goes for my plan, it'll be no problem. I'm sure I can help you," said Dave. "Tell you what, I'll probably be tied up the rest of the afternoon, but why don't we meet here at the end of the day and we can talk."

When Art, Mac, and Wendy quit work that day, Dave was waiting for them by the Main Gate.

"How did everything go in your meeting with the King?" Wendy asked.

"Not as well as I'd hoped," said Dave. "The King is, you know, kind of skeptical. He kept singing the blues about how the treasure chest is nearly empty and he doesn't want to risk any gold on something new. So I guess I'll be heading on down the road."

"Whoa! Wait!" said Wendy. "We need your help!"

"Yeah," said Art, "don't forget we saved your life."

"The least you can do is cast one spell for us," said Mac.

"Well, what kind of spell did you have in mind?" asked Dave. "I mean, what are you trying to accomplish?"

The arrow-makers told Dave their story, all about the dragon threat, and their need to double the number of Magic Arrows for the knights, and how they needed to get the other arrow-makers involved in making the whole Tower improve, and how they had failed.

Dave considered this. "All right, I've got some magic that can help," he said. "And I suppose my life is worth at least one spell."

"Now you're talking," said Mac. Then he pointed at Tower Two. "Well, there it is, that's where we work. Wave your wand or whatever you do."

"Ah, sorry, but that's not the way my magic works," said Dave.

"It's not?"

"No, I'm not the one who casts the spells."

"If you don't, who does?"

"You, the workers, do. This is magic you perform on your own."

"But we're not wizards," said Art.

"You don't have to be."

"I don't know about this," said Mac. "Personally, I've never cast a spell before."

"Okay, but I'll tell you one thing for sure," said Dave. "I can't work this magic for you. You have to do it for yourselves."

Art, Mac, and Wendy looked at one another.

"All right," said Wendy. "Let's give it a try."

Dave took them aside. "The spell I'm going to teach you is called the Three Keys Spell."

"Oooo!" said Art. "That sounds like a good one! What kind of wand do we need?"

"To cast this spell, you don't need a wand or a scroll or magic dust or anything else," said Dave. "You cast this spell by the way you behave with the people around you. Now, to get you started, I'm going to give you something to remember always."

"What's that?"

"The Golden Rule."

"The Golden Rule?"

"That's right," said Dave. "In all your dealings with other workers in the castle, follow the Golden Rule. Do you know what that means?"

"Well," said Art, "it means you're supposed to do unto others ... well, basically, you treat other people the way that you, yourself, would prefer to be treated."

"Exactly," said Dave, "and this is the key to the Three Keys Spell. Now listen closely. ... "

And he taught them the Three Keys Spell.

By the time Dave was done, it was nearly sunset.

"Okay, good luck," he said. "Got a busy day tomorrow, so I've got to go. Just hope I don't run into any more dragons on the way back."

"Back to where?" asked Art.

"Back to where I come from, the normal world."

"The normal world? Where's that?"

"Not that far away. It's just hard to get to. So long!"

And he waved good-bye.

"Wait a minute!" said Wendy. "What if this magic isn't enough?"

"Yeah, what if we need to talk to you again?" asked Art.

Dave frowned. "I was afraid you were going to ask that. Communication between my world and yours is very difficult, and I don't plan to be back in this area for quite a while."

"I don't blame you, after you nearly got eaten," said Mac.

"Tell you what I'll do, though," said Dave. He opened his briefcase and took out a small wooden chest, which he handed to Art Halegiver. Naturally, Art tried to open the chest, but he could not. It was locked.

"If you're serious, and you practice the Three Keys Spell and learn it well," said Dave, "you'll be empowered enough to open the chest."

"What's inside?" asked Art.

"All the magic you'll need until I get back."

"But ... but—"

"Don't worry, you're smart people. You can figure it out."

With that, Dave tapped his briefcase seven times, snapped his fingers, and in a burst of light that seemed to contain every color of the spectrum, he was gone.

7

The next day, up in the Arrowhead Area, Mac was at work when his helper, Dilbert Dooley, brought him some of the special metal from which the arrowheads were made.

Now, in order to work with the metal, it had to be a certain temperature, designated as "HO-HO-HOT!" and it was Dilbert's job to make sure this was so. But with one blow of his hammer, Mac could tell that the metal was only "Ho-Hum Hot."

All day long, Mac had been trying sincerely to follow the Golden Rule and do what Dave the Zapp! Wizard had prescribed in order to cast the Three Keys Spell.

So Mac had done his best to be pleasant, and it had not been too difficult, because there had not been any problems—until now.

What Mac wanted to do was what he usually did when Dilbert made a mistake, which was to yell at him something like "Dilbert, you bonehead! You have the brains of a fence post! Don't you know HO-HO-HOT metal when you see it? Are you deliberately trying to screw me up, or is this just another of your stupid mistakes?"

But he looked up and saw the note he had nailed to the wall that morning. This was the note he had written to himself while talking to Dave so he would remember how to cast the Three Keys Spell.

Part of the note read ...

Three Keys Spell

Cast the Three Keys Spell
By Behaving Toward Others
According to These Principles:

1. Maintain or enhance self-esteem.

Now, much as Mac wanted to, shouting insults certainly would not maintain or enhance Dilbert's self-esteem.

So at first, Mac thought, I'll just pretend the problem never happened; when Dilbert has his back turned, I'll reheat the metal myself.

Then, remembering the Golden Rule, he thought, Wait a minute, how would I want to be treated if I made a mistake? Would I want someone fixing my mistakes behind my back and not telling me about them?

And the honest answer was, no. He would not want to be treated that way. He would want to be told about the mistake and allowed to correct it on his own—but told in a way that didn't make him feel low or worth less as a person for having made the mistake.

So instead of either yelling or ignoring what had happened, Mac simply said, "Dilbert, I think there is a problem with this metal. Usually you give me metal that's the right temperature, but this batch doesn't seem to be hot enough."

By putting it this way, Mac made it clear that the problem was with the object, the metal, and not with the person. In other words, Mac maintained Dilbert's self-esteem.

Dilbert was not the brightest guy in the world, but like all of us, he basically wanted to do a good job. He looked at the metal and said, "Sorry, Mac, we've been having some trouble with the furnace. Let me reheat it right away."

As Dilbert took the metal back to the furnace, a small bolt of lightning appeared out of nowhere and flashed between Mac and his coworker.

Zapp!

Well, how about that, Mac thought. Maybe there is something to this magic.

From then on, whether there were problems or not, Mac did his best in his dealings with his coworkers to make sure they kept feeling okay about themselves. He treated people with respect. He gave them credit for things they did right.

When there were problems, Mac tried as he spoke to people to separate the problem from the person—as he had done with Dilbert. Even when something happened that made Mac angry, he tried to make it clear that his anger was over the problem, not the person.

And whenever they were deserved, Mac tried to say things that would also enhance the other arrow-makers' self-esteem. These were not so much comments like "Gee, that's a nice shirt you're wearing," but remarks that would build pride, like "That was a good job, Dilbert. We hammered out twenty-four heads today!"

Now, this was not always easy for Mac, because he saw himself as a tough guy. And myth has it that tough guys are not supposed to concern themselves with things like feelings and other people's self-esteem.

Being tough, though, Mac made himself observe these principles. Because there really was a payoff. Over time those little Zapps that Mac gave out began to connect people to one another.

And slowly other head-shapers began to follow Mac's example and return the Zapp's he gave out. They became more than a bunch of individuals making arrowheads. They became a group of people who wanted to do good work together, united by this mysterious energy called ...

Zapp!

Meanwhile, down in the Shaftshop on that first day of trying to use the Three Keys Spell, Art had somewhat the opposite problem than Mac.

Art found himself on the receiving end of criticism.

There he was, minding his business, when Fernanda came in and gave Art a piece of her mind.

Fernanda worked on the Feather Floor gluing feathers onto the arrow shafts received from the Shaftshop.

She came straight to Art because he was the handiest and said, "Look, I'm going nuts and it's all your fault! It's just plain crazy! We've got so many bundles of arrow shafts upstairs I can't even close the door!"

Now, Art had little patience with complainers, especially complainers who made the problem sound like it was Art's fault.

Ordinarily, Art might have put her off by saying something like "Yeah, yeah, I'll see what I can do." Or "If you'd try a little harder, you wouldn't have this problem." Or he might have just kept on working and ignored her.

But today he looked up and read the note he had made the night before, when talking to Dave about the Three Keys Spell. And the middle of the note read ...

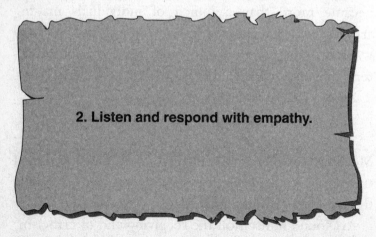

2. Listen and respond with empathy.

So instead of ignoring Fernanda and her complaint, Art instead stopped what he was doing and faced her.

He listened to what she was saying and genuinely tried to understand her. Which was not easy, because she had not organized her thinking and the words and phrases spilled out of her mouth however her brain randomly fetched them.

When she was done, Art repeated to her a summary of what he thought she had said: "As I understand it, you don't want all the arrow shafts we produce down here to show up on your floor when we've finished them. You want them to show up when you need them. Is that right?"

Yes, that was factually correct. But that really was not all that Fernanda wanted.

When people try to communicate, they not only want to be factually understood, they also want an appropriate emotional response from the person who is supposed to be listening. In short, they want something called *empathy*.

Empathy, Art had learned from Wizard Dave, was understanding and being sensitive to what another person has gone through—even though that person may not communicate his or her thoughts and feelings explicitly.

So Art said to her, "You sound like you're very upset and frustrated by this. It's a real problem for you, isn't it?"

"Yes, it is," said Fernanda. "I feel totally overwhelmed. And thank you for trying to understand."

Zapp!

As a result of Art's listening and then responding with empathy, a tiny bolt of lightning flashed between the two arrow-makers.

At the top of the Tower, Wendy was having her own troubles that day.

One of them was that the wands the magic workers used to impart their technical spells to the arrows had to be recharged on a regular basis. But Wendy was discovering that not all of the wands were finding their way to the magic recharger.

Time and again she would pick up a wand to add magic to a fresh batch of arrows—and the wand would be dead, all of its magic exhausted.

In the past, Wendy either would have put up with the problem or would have tried to solve it all by herself.

But today she glanced up at the note above her desk that had Wizard Dave's Three Keys Spell on it. And at the bottom, it read ...

3. Ask for help and encourage involvement.

So rather than ignore the problem or solve the problem alone, she instead went to a couple of her magic coworkers, Zachary and Krystal.

"I'd like to get your help on something," she said. "I know we're all having a problem with the wands not being fully charged. So I thought maybe if we all put our heads together we can come up with a solution. ... "

Zapp!

Wendy asked Zachary and Krystal for their help and got them involved.

Of course, the other arrow-makers were not blind. They could see the flashes of Zapp! lightning as well as Mac, Art, or Wendy. Even if the Zapp! had been invisible, they would have known that something good was happening, because they knew they felt better. Whatever this "Zapp!" was, it had to be powerful, they knew that for sure.

Naturally, they were curious. "Hey, how'd you do that?" they would ask.

So whenever the opportunity came up, the three friends showed their coworkers the principles of the Three Keys Spell and taught them how to cast it. And as more and more of the other arrow-makers of Tower Two learned how to cast the Three Keys Spell, the power of the Zapp! became multiplied.

Three Keys Spell

Cast the Three Keys Spell
By Behaving Toward Others
According to These Principles:

1. Maintain or enhance self-esteem.

2. Listen and respond with empathy.

3. Ask for help and encourage involvement.

One of the nicest things about the Three Keys Spell was that an arrow-maker could use the third key to ask for help and yet be assured of not losing face. In the past, many of the arrow-makers had been reluctant to ask for help—from either the Boss or anyone else—because it was thought to be a sign of weakness.

But now it was understood that if you asked for help, the other arrow-makers would respond using the first two keys. If other people are maintaining your self-esteem, listening, and responding with empathy when you ask for help, you don't have much to worry about.

Zapp!

Now, of course not everyone remembered to use the spell 100 percent of the time. Occasionally there were still arguments and bad feelings. Still, the arrow-makers used the spell often enough that the Zapps were soon arcing back and forth among the arrow-makers with great regularity. Even when there were disagreements, the Three Keys Spell enabled the arrow-makers to get past their anger and frustration a lot faster.

One of the really smart things that the arrow-makers of Tower Two did was to use the Three Keys Spell in their dealings with the Boss. Art, Mac, and Wendy started it, and others slowly learned to do this as well.

For instance, when the Boss made a good decision that helped the arrow-makers handle the workload better or made the day go smoother, they would tell her about it. One or several of the arrow-makers would say to the Boss, "That was a good one." Or "That was a smart call," and give her a thumbs-up, while explaining exactly what the Boss had done that helped.

Zapp!

You see, the Boss had a need for self-esteem just like any other worker in the castle. When the arrow-makers maintained or built her self-esteem, the Boss was inclined to return the favor.

Zapp!

Unfortunately, one of the reasons why the Boss was not the best boss in the Magic World was that she was not very good at communicating her thinking and her concerns.

By using the second key with the Boss, listening and responding with empathy, the arrow-makers often were able to show the Boss that they understood a decision and why she had made a call the way she had—even when they didn't totally agree with it.

One day the Boss came into the Shaftshop and began ranting and raving about some perfectly good pieces of shaft stock she had found in the trash.

Though he was angry about her ranting and raving, Art Halegiver stopped, listened to what the Boss was saying, put himself in her place for a moment, and said, "Wow, you're really upset about this, aren't you?"

"You bet I am," said the Boss.

Art thought for a moment and said, "You know, Boss, I've never seen you so bent out of shape about something like this. Is it because you're under a lot of pressure to make the Tower stay within budget this year?"

"Well ... yes. That's exactly it," said the Boss. "Thanks for trying to understand my position."

Zapp!

And the third key came in handy when the arrow-makers discussed with the Boss the solutions to their problems.

For instance, Art and several of the shaft-turners went to the Boss and said, "We have a problem with the shaft stock and we'd appreciate your help as we try to solve it."

"Sure," said the Boss, "what do you have in mind?"

"The reason why you've been finding pieces of shaft stock in the trash is that a couple of the woodcutters have been giving us stock with knots in the middle. What looks like good stock on the surface really isn't. So we'd like your ideas on what we should do about this ...

Zapp!

The thing the arrow-makers especially liked about using the third key was that they weren't asking the Boss to take over the problem and solve it for them. They were getting ideas and assistance from the Boss so that they could do a better job solving the problem on their own.

You see, while it might seem terrific to have someone else solve your problems for you, in fact you lose something important. You lose the pride of being responsible. You miss out on the victory of solving the problem.

By using the third key, though, they got the Boss's

participation, but kept their pride. When the solution to the problem was at hand, it was the arrow-makers, not the Boss, who owned it. Which in turn entitled them to the pride of accomplishment.

Zapp!

In time, some amazing things happened as the Zapp! bolts circulated through Tower Two. On the practical side, work went smoother and people got along better. This in itself made the shaft-turners, the head-shapers, and the wand-wavers able to get more work done. And simple problems in each of these areas got worked out faster—often without having to go to the Boss.

Aside from that, the workday was always nicer when there was some Zapp! in the air. Some of the arrow-makers actually began to look forward to coming to work.

But some magical things began to happen as well. One of the strangest had to do with these metal keys that would appear unexpectedly in the pockets of the arrow-makers.

"What are these?" Wendy asked the others, showing them a bronze key, a silver key, and a gold key—each with a little lightning bolt on it. "I have no idea where they came from or what they're for."

"I don't know, but I've got the same three keys," said Mac.

"Me, too," said Art, producing his three. "I've tried them in all the locks in the Tower and none of them fit."

"I wonder if they have something to do with the spell," suggested Wendy. "If that wizard, Dave, ever stops back, we'll have to ask him if he knows what these are for."

All at once, the three friends had the same thought.

"The chest!" they said in unison.

It had been some time since Dave's visit, and they had all but forgotten the wooden chest he had left with them. Art had kept it under his workbench. Together now, they rushed down to the Shaftshop, took out the chest, dusted off the shaft shavings, and examined it.

Indeed, there were three small lock holes in the front.

"Who should open it?" asked Wendy.

"He gave it to Art," said Mac. "I think Art should try first."

With a shrug of his shoulders, Art Halegiver produced from his pocket the bronze, silver and gold keys for which he had previously been unable to find a practical use.

One by one, he fit the three keys into the locks, turned each one—and as each lock opened, the key that had turned it disappeared. But when Art opened the third lock, the lid of the chest clicked and popped up slightly.

Art lifted the lid, and a small, bright ball of light floated out of the chest, drifted to the ceiling and bounced around up there, and began to expand until it filled the room with a weak but warm light.

Puzzled, Art peered into the chest again, expecting

to find it empty, but instead he found there was another slightly smaller wooden chest inside.

Art removed the smaller chest and gave it to Mac, whereupon Mac used his three keys to open it. Same thing happened. A small, bright ball of light floated out and began to expand, giving a weak, warm light. And inside the smaller chest was a still smaller chest. Mac removed it and gave it to Wendy.

She used her three keys—and again the same thing happened. There was still another chest to be opened, but they were out of keys.

"Now what do we do?" asked Wendy.

"Let's see if any of the other arrow-makers have keys," suggested Art.

"I know my helper, Dilbert, has his three keys," said Mac.

So they took the unopened chest to Dilbert, who opened it. Guess what? Another ball of light and another small, locked wooden chest were inside.

"When are we going to get some diamonds and rubies?" complained Mac.

Instead there was always a ball of light and yet another chest, which they would give to another arrow-maker who had earned three keys.

When they ran out of people who had the three keys, they would teach the spell to new people, if for no other reason than to be able to open the next locked chest. Eventually, everybody in all of Tower Two learned the Three Keys Spell, even the feather-gluers and twine-tiers.

To everyone's amazement, there were enough wooden chests to go around, one for each of the arrow-makers of Tower Two—until finally there was a chest with four locks.

On the lid of the last chest was an inscription, which read: "To Be Opened by the Boss."

They took this chest to the Boss. They explained what had happened. And then they taught *her* the Three Keys Spell.

In the next few days, as the Boss used the spell in her dealings with the arrow-makers, she, too, earned a bronze key, a silver key, and a gold key.

But there were four locks on the chest marked for her, and without a fourth key, the chest would not open.

"Great!" said Mac in exasperation. "What a waste of time that was!"

"I don't think so," said Art. "Take a look around."

It had happened so gradually, no one had noticed right away. But all of those small, bright balls of light had slowly joined with one another and filled the entire Tower, becoming brighter and stronger as they overlapped with one another. Now some of the darkness, dreariness, and fog of working in Tower Two had begun to lift. Inside it was like morning following night.

"You're right!" said Wendy. "It's all changed! It's not gray anymore. Everything has changed! It's—"

"PINK!" said Mac.

8

For the first time anyone could remember, Tower Two was a color other than gray. And with the possible exception of Mac, who was not wild about pink, everyone in Tower Two thought the new color was terrific. But even Mac had to admit that, after looking at plain gray for so many years, pink wasn't so bad.

Fortunately for Mac and other tough guys in the Tower, the pink matured. It became red. A deeper, brighter, energetic, full-of-promise red. It was the shade of red at early dawn on a new day.

There was just one problem, the same old problem as before:

The total number of Magic Arrows coming out of Tower Two was pretty much the same as always.

Even the Three Keys Spell had not changed that fact. Output had not improved.

Meanwhile, out on the horizon, the dragons were circling. Used to be the dragons would keep their distance from the castle. Not anymore; the scaly beasts were plainly visible from every window of every tower.

Every hour of the day and night, the trumpets on the battlements blared, sounding the alarm, calling the knights to mount up and charge to the rescue.

Finally it was confirmed, there were indeed more dragons showing up in Lamron than ever before. There were several reasons. One was the dreaded Dragon Moon that was approaching. But another was that the other castles had become so much more effective at fighting dragons that more and more of the monsters were coming to Lamron, where the pickings were relatively easy.

The news just got worse and worse.

Word came that Castle Colossal was offering three months of free dragon-fighting services to all new settlers.

And over to the west, the castle of Count Discount was offering prices that were 10 percent below those of Lamron Castle, plus double coupons!

These were great deals—deals that the King of Lamron Castle might have matched or exceeded in better times. But the castle could not match them now because of the gold shortage.

Then one morning one of the castle criers went through each tower shouting: "Important message from the King: Try harder! Work smarter! Do better! Important message from the King … !"

"What's that all about?" asked Mac.

"That's the *New, Improved* Quick Improvement Program," said Wendy.

"Terrific," said Art. "Why don't we just go out to the dragons and ask them to go away?"

"But you can't say the Three Keys Spell has worked any better," argued Mac.

"What do you mean? Of course it's working! Everybody's Zapped! We're all charged up, the whole Tower is a nice rosy red, and we've never gotten along better with the Boss!" said Art.

"True," said Mac, "but the plain truth of the matter is that we're not turning out any more Magic Arrows now than we were before."

And they knew this almost certainly to be true because Wendy's count of finished arrows at the top of the Tower had still not increased, even though she and the other wand-wavers were finishing well before quitting time every afternoon. They simply were not getting the arrows from the lower floors of the Tower.

"But, wait, I have an idea," said Wendy. "Let's use the Three Keys Spell to get everyone involved in this."

"Get everyone involved?"

"Yes, get the others involved in reaching the goal we set for ourselves—doubling the number of arrows for the knights," she said. "We'll use the third key of the Three Keys Spell. We'll ask for their help and involve them in decisions. That way, we can work on problems not just locally in our own little work areas, but throughout the whole Tower. Maybe we can figure out some ways to make the flow of arrows move faster."

"Great idea," said Art.

Because it was her idea, Wendy was the one who went to the Boss to get permission for the big meeting.

Very excited, she rushed into the Boss's office and blurted out, "Guess what! I've got this great idea! We're all going to take a day off, everybody in the whole

Tower, and get together someplace and have a good talk about all our problems!"

Then—expecting the Boss to jump up and down and say, "Yes! Yes! Do it! Take the day off!"—Wendy went on to describe in great detail the refreshments she had planned for the meeting. She was in the middle of relating her recipe for fruit punch when she noticed the Boss was not jumping up and down with excitement to match her own; instead, the Boss was shaking her head.

"I don't think so," said the Boss.

"But, but … how can you say no to such a great idea?"

"Sorry, but I just did," said the Boss.

Wendy was crushed. She ran to the top of the Tower and sulked, refusing to talk to anyone for the rest of the day.

"Did you hear about Wendy?" asked Mac.

"No, what?" asked Art.

"The Boss didn't like her idea."

"Gee, that's too bad. I thought it was pretty good myself," said Art.

"Yeah, I thought so, too," said Mac. "But I guess that's the end of it."

By habit now, Art Halegiver was still trying to improve his work and his work area. He had come up with a new idea, but he needed more space to implement it. As he was thinking about what he could get rid of so as to make space, his eyes fell upon the original wooden chest that Wizard Dave had given them.

After opening it, Art had kept the chest because he had no good reason to throw it away. But now it was taking up most of a shelf and he decided it had to go.

He picked it up, carried it to the trash bin, was about to pitch it, and—by habit—checked to see that it was empty.

It was not.

Down at the bottom, unnoticed some days ago in the excitement of removing the smaller chest, was a dog-eared, dusty little book with a lightning bolt on the cover, entitled:

A little while later, Art ran up the steps to the top of the Tower, burst into the Magic Room, and said, "Hey, Wendy, check this out!"

Still depressed, Wendy pretended she was not interested.

"I know you're still upset," said Art, "but, look ... I found some magic to help you get your idea accepted."

He showed her the page he had been reading.

Magic Brew to Enhance Acceptance When Presenting Ideas to Bosses

Start With: 1 Good Idea.

Include Satisfactory Answers to the Following:

★ **Which organizational goals or values are supported by my ideas?**

★ **What are the benefits and costs of my idea?**

★ **What incentive will the Boss have for saying "yes"?**

★ **What will the Boss's objections most likely be?**

★ **What can I say in response if the Boss voices those objections?**

★ **What are some alternatives if the Boss won't buy my idea "as is"?**

Apply Ample Zapps from Three Keys
Spell as Needed.

So Wendy studied this page from *The Zapp! Wizard's Spell Book,* then went back to the Boss and presented her suggestion again.

This time she was careful to include the goal of Tower Two and the likely benefit of what would be accomplished (more arrows) and the expected cost (a few hours of time). She was also careful to stick to the main points of her idea and not get sidetracked into details that the Boss wasn't likely to care about (like refreshments).

Well, the Boss still said, "No."

But Wendy hung in there and asked if the Boss would reveal her objections.

"My concern," said the Boss, "is that if all of you arrow-makers spend your time in meetings, nobody is going to be working on the arrows."

However, Wendy had anticipated that the Boss might say something like this. And she used the second key of the Three Keys Spell. She listened, then responded with empathy.

"Boss, we know you're very worried about how much work gets done," said Wendy, "and so are we." (*Zapp!*) "The whole idea of holding the meeting is to get more done in the long run. But we can't do that unless you give us the time to solve problems."

She could see the Boss was reconsidering. "But why do you need everybody in the whole Tower to be in this meeting?"

"Because we need everybody to know they have to be part of the solution," said Wendy. "In order for the whole Tower to improve, it takes more than a few individuals."

"Okay, I'll buy that," said the Boss, "but the feather-gluers and the twine-tiers are way behind in their work. If we take them off the job for a meeting, it means fewer arrows."

"But if we can deal with the problems that are holding us up, you will see a gain that more than makes up for the time we spend on this."

"All right, but if you have too many people in the meeting," said the Boss, "it's going to be very difficult for you to manage."

"Okay, then why don't we start by having one person from each work group in the Tower meet with us?" Wendy suggested, using one of her preplanned alternatives.

"Good. I like it," said the Boss.

And she approved Wendy's idea.

A day or so later, for the first time ever, people from all five of the functions of arrow-making sat down together to attack problems that were holding them up.

Art represented the shaft-turners and Mac the head-shapers. From the Feather Floor came Fernanda. And from Twine-Tying came a little old man named Gramps.

"We know you're all serious arrow-makers," said Wendy, using the first key of the Three Keys Spell, then invoking the third: "And so we'd like your help in solving some problems."

Zapp!

Well, Gramps and Fernanda jumped right in.

"I'll tell you the first problem we ought to solve," said Fernanda. "Not enough space!"

"You can say that again," said Gramps. "Up in Twine-Tying, I hardly have room to turn around! And it's all your fault, you workaholics down in Shaft-Turning and Head-Shaping! You're making more shafts and heads than we can handle!"

"That's right," said Fernanda. "And I want to know what you're going to do about it."

Wendy, Mac, and Art all looked at one another, unsure of what they had gotten themselves into. Already this seemed to be on a bad track.

"I'll tell you what we need," said Gramps. "We need a big storeroom. Then we can take all these extra arrowheads and arrow shafts and stuff them in there until we get a chance to work on them."

"Great minds think alike, Gramps," said Fernanda. "That's exactly what I was going to suggest."

Weeks later, the arrow-makers had drawn up elaborate plans for the greatest storeroom in the history of Lamron Castle. They had considered everything: how many arrow parts it would hold, how many torches they would need for lighting, which walls would have to be taken out to make room for it, right down to how many sledgehammers and chisels they would need for demolition.

They took this proposal to the Boss. And the Boss totally freaked out. In her anger and exasperation, she forgot all about the Three Keys Spell and yelled:

"You spent all this time and effort … *on a storeroom?!* How is a *storeroom* going to help us build even one more Magic Arrow for the knights?"

And with this, much of the rosy warm light of Tower Two began to fade back to gray.

It did not take long, however, for the Boss to change her tune. Because on her desk was a letter from the Duke of Arrows to all arrow-making Tower bosses.

"The Dragon Moon is fast approaching," said the duke's letter. "How are you all coming along on your required 10 percent improvement?"

The Boss glanced at her Quick Improvement Program calendar, and indeed the encircled date of the Dragon Moon was not far off. The plain fact of the matter was that if she was going to satisfy the duke's demand for improvement, she couldn't do it alone.

Maybe I should give them another chance, the Boss thought. These days a boss needs help from everybody.

That same day, the Boss called the five arrow-makers back and talked to them.

"Even though you got offtrack, and even though some time was wasted, I would still appreciate your help in solving the problem of the Magic Arrow backlog," said the Boss. "This time, even though I'm very busy, I'll try to stay in closer touch with you."

This was some comfort to the arrow-makers. But not much.

Late in the afternoon, Art, Mac, and Wendy got together to talk over what they were going to do.

"I don't care what she says," said Mac. "Next time *we* are going to make sure the Boss knows what's going on. I'm not going to have my time—our time—wasted like that again."

"Personally, I'm more worried about something else," said Wendy. "I'm worried about how it was so easy for us to get offtrack."

"You want to know what happened? We never thought through the problem," said Mac. "We saw a symptom and jumped straight to a solution—before we ever defined the real problem!" Then he added, "Of course I knew that all along."

"You knew all along? Then why didn't you say something!" said Wendy.

Mac lowered his face. "I didn't want to hurt their feelings—Gramps and Fernanda, that is. I figured that if I told them their idea about the storeroom stunk like a skunk, they'd get all huffy and we'd never get them to cooperate on the real problem. So I just let it slide."

"Next time, Mac, speak up," said Wendy. "But don't tell them their idea stinks. Use the first two keys of the Three Keys Spell to tell them the truth in a way that they don't feel insulted."

"Yeah, yeah, I know," said Mac. "But assuming there's going to be a next time, how are we going to do this so that the real problem gets solved?" He turned to Art. "What do you think, Art? You haven't said a word yet."

Art Halegiver looked up from *The Zapp! Wizard's Spell Book.*

"Hey, Art, get your nose out of that book," said Mac, "and help us figure out what we're going to do."

"Wait a minute, I've found it!"

"Found what?"

"I knew he'd have a spell for this," said Art. "It's called the ACTION Spell for problem solving and solution implementation. We're going to cast this spell and then we're going to stay on track next time."

So the arrow-makers tried again.

The Zapp! Wizard's Spell Book

The ACTION Spell
Use to Solve Problems and Implement Solutions

To Cast the ACTION Spell:

1. **A**ssess Situation and Define Problem.
2. Determine **C**auses.
3. **T**arget Solutions and Develop Ideas.
4. **I**mplement Ideas.
5. Make it an **ON**going Process.

IMPORTANT: Be Sure to *Involve Others* While Casting Each Step of This Spell!

And this time when they all sat down together, they invoked the ACTION Spell. Mac opened by casting the first part of it.

He said, "First of all, let's assess the situation and define the problem." Then he involved the others by asking them to contribute their observations.

"The situation as I see it," said Art, "is that heads and shafts are piling up on the Feather Floor and in Twine-Tying because they're not getting through these steps fast enough."

"Well, that's not our fault!" Fernanda said defensively.

"We're not saying anyone is to blame," said Wendy, maintaining Fernanda's self-esteem. (*Zapp!*) "We just want to figure out what exactly is going on."

"The result," said Art, "is that Tower Two is unable to increase production of the Magic Arrows the knights desperately need to defeat the dragons."

After some discussion, they all agreed that this was the problem.

"Then let's talk about what is causing this," said Art.

They talked about the suspected causes and eventually agreed that the head-shapers and the shaft-turners had increased their output, but as yet the twine-tiers and the feather-gluers had not kept pace with the improvements and so had become a bottleneck.

Now that they had gotten through the second step of the ACTION Spell, determining causes, they moved on to the third.

Wendy did this by saying, "Let's try to figure out a solution by coming up with some ideas."

"Now, we are all aware that everyone in Twine-Tying and Feather-Gluing is working hard," said Art, saying this to maintain the self-esteem of Gramps and Fernanda (*Zapp!*), "but we need a smart solution to this problem. Do you have any ideas on this?"

Here it got a bit sticky.

Fernanda had what she thought was a terrific idea to solve the problem. "Quit sending us so much extra work! We can't handle it all! The head-shapers and the shaft-turners should cut back!"

At this, Mac invoked the second of the Three Keys. He listened to her, then he said (with empathy), "Fernanda, I know you wish that things could go back to being like they always were. We all wish that from time to time. However, that's just not going to work. If we can't make more Magic Arrows, we're all going to be in big trouble."

At this, Gramps spoke up. "I'll tell you what we need: We need more hands! More hands to do the tying and more hands to do the gluing! It's as simple as that."

Of course, it was not as simple as that—though this, too, seemed like a great idea at first. They broke from the meeting, went to the Boss and asked her about Gramps's idea.

"Well, believe me, I would hire more people if I could," said the Boss. "But the King has issued an edict: no more hiring until the gold stops draining out of the treasure chest. And, anyway, if I hire more people our costs go up, and if our costs go up our prices have to go up. That's not going to help us convince citizens across the countryside that they should stay in Lamron."

So the arrow-makers had to think of other possible solutions. Then it occurred to Art Halegiver that in one sense, Fernanda was right. The Tower as a whole could not use 100 percent of the output that the head-shapers and shaft-turners were now capable of.

Art mentioned this and said, "Why don't the head-shapers and shaft-turners help out the twine-tiers and the feather-gluers for part of the day whenever there is a backlog of unfinished arrows?"

Now, this may seem like an obvious and logical thing to do. But as is so often the case with the obvious and logical, this was a radical departure from the norm for the arrow-makers.

"What?! Why, that's never been done before!" said Gramps. "Twine-tying is a fine and ancient art. It can't be done by just … anybody!"

"That goes double for feather-gluing," said Fernanda, "which is an even finer and more ancient art."

"Then why don't you teach the rest of us these fine and ancient arts—or at least enough about them so that we can help you?" suggested Wendy.

"Hmmm … hadn't thought of that," said Gramps, though the idea somewhat appealed to him.

"Actually, I would appreciate the help," said Fernanda.

"Well, I don't know. Twine-tying is mighty tricky," said Gramps. Then he thought for a minute. "On the other hand, if we don't solve this problem, we'll all be cooked. Okay, why not give it a try."

And this is what they agreed to do. Remembering what had happened last time, though, they now checked with the Boss before they went further.

"I think it's a fine solution," said the Boss. And she offered some ideas to them.

Zapp!

Now came the fourth part of the ACTION Spell: Implement the idea. They worked out a schedule in which the head-shapers and shaft-turners would work six hours at their normal jobs and two hours a day at either twine-tying or feather-gluing.

Then they agreed how they would monitor how the plan was working and continue to look for other ways to improve. This was the fifth and final step of the ACTION Spell: Make the process ongoing.

When they had finished, everyone felt good. This was first time that different groups of arrow-makers had sat down together and worked out a solution to a problem on their own. And it was a tremendous charge.

Zapp!

When Art, Mac, Wendy, Fernanda, and Gramps returned to Tower Two, there was another color added to red. This time it was orange.

9

For a couple of days Art, Mac, and Wendy thought they had solved the problem and now everything would be fine.

But it soon became apparent that they were the only ones in the Tower taking their turns helping out the twine-tiers and feather-gluers.

"Hey, this isn't fair!" Wendy complained. "What's wrong with everybody else? How come they're not helping?"

Neither Art nor Mac had an answer.

"We ought to have the Boss yell at everybody and *make* them help out," said Wendy.

"Sure, but you know what would happen," said Art. "After a day or two the Boss would get tired of yelling. As soon as she stopped yelling, they'd quit helping."

"I don't get it," said Mac. "In the long run, it's in their own best interest to make this solution work. Why aren't they doing it voluntarily?"

"There must be something wrong with the magic," said Wendy. "It's not working."

So Art went back and reread the ACTION Spell.

"The trouble isn't in the spell," Art told them. "The trouble is in the way we cast it."

"Why? What did we do wrong?" asked Mac.

"Remember what happened," said Art. "After we came up with the schedule, we took the copies back to our areas and we tacked them to the wall."

"What's wrong with that?"

"We didn't involve the others," said Art. "We put a schedule on the wall and expected everyone else to follow it. That's not the way the magic works. It was our solution and our schedule—not theirs. I think that's why they're not helping."

"Where does that leave us?" asked Wendy. "Do we have to start all over again?"

"No, but we do have to get them involved somehow," said Art.

So they went back to each group of arrow-makers. They asked for their help and had the other arrow-makers come up with *their own* way to implement the solution and develop *their own* schedules.

This time the magic worked. People started helping.

Zapp!

For a week the bundles of arrow shafts and the buckets of arrowheads slowly went down. Wendy found she had to skip her turn in Twine-Tying because she and the other wand-wavers now had enough work to keep them busy for most of the day.

But by the end of two weeks, the bundles and buckets began to rise again.

One day Art noticed that his friend Mac, who was supposed to be in Twine-Tying for two hours every afternoon, was not showing up. And, unlike Wendy, Mac had no good reason not to be there.

So Art went to Mac and said, "What gives? You didn't show up when you were scheduled to."

"Well, I've got a sore finger, smacked it with my hammer," said Mac. "You can't expect me to tie twine with a sore finger, can you?"

This was a reasonable excuse, Art allowed. But then Mac's sore finger never seemed to heal. Pretty soon all of the head-shapers were getting sore fingers.

Then Art discovered that a similar malady was afflicting the shaft-turners. They kept getting cut by splinters. But only on the days when they were supposed to help with feather-gluing, no other time.

"All right, Mac, what's going on?" Art asked one day at lunch. "How come you and the other head-shapers aren't helping the twine-tiers?"

"I told you already, we've got sore fingers!"

"No, there's another reason than that," said Art.

"All right, I'll admit it. I don't like working in Twine-Tying."

"What don't you like?"

"Look, I'm a head-shaper, not a twine-tier!" Mac exploded. "I am paid to shape arrowheads, not fiddle with string! Twine-tying is the dullest, most boring work I've ever done! And the twine-tiers are the dullest, most boring people I've ever worked with!"

"But, Mac," Wendy said, "we're arrow-makers *first* and head-shapers, shaft-turners, twine-tiers second. Can't you see how important it is to help out the others?"

"Sure, but you've worked in Twine-Tying," said Mac. "Did you like working there?"

"No, I hated every minute of it," Wendy admitted.

"How come?" asked Art.

"For one thing, all the twine-tiers made me feel stupid because I didn't know what to do."

"Yeah, and the worst of them is that old geezer Gramps," said Mac. "He's so crotchety, he just waits for us screw up so that he can look good."

"Well," said Art, "I can tell you it's no better on the Feather Floor. If Fernanda tells me one more time I've glued the feathers on upside down, I'm going to … " He shook his head, sat back in his seat, and let out a disgusted sigh.

"It makes me mad," said Mac. "Here we are trying to help them out and they won't give us any *support!*"

Art sat straight again. "What did you say?"

"I said, they won't give us any support."

"That's it!" said Art, and he got up and left, saying, "I'll be back."

He came back flipping through the pages of *The Zapp! Wizard's Spell Book.*

"Here it is," he said. "I knew I'd seen something in here about it."

"About what?"

"Support!" said Art. "Look, here it is. 'The Master Spell of Support.'"

Mac and Wendy peered over Art's shoulder.

"It looks a lot more complicated than the other spells," said Wendy.

"Not really," said Art. "It's just that because it's a Master Spell, it has three spells that work together."

"Let's try it," said Mac. "What have we got to lose?"

The Zapp! Wizard's Spell Book

The Master Spell of Support

Spell #1: Coaching Spell

Spell #2: Guide-Through-Feedback Spell

Spell #3: Encouragement Spell

The next morning, Art and Mac went to see Gramps in the Twine-Tying room.

"Say, Gramps, I hear that in your day you were the Castle's best ball player," said Art. "Is that right?"

Gramps immediately brightened at the compliment and the memories and said, "You bet. Why, there was no one who could top me."

"No kidding," said Art. "Tell me, how'd you get to be so good?"

"Natural talent, of course," said Gramps, who was not known for modesty.

"I'm sure that was partly it," said Art, "but how did you develop that talent?"

"Well ... practice. And I had a couple of good coaches, my own pappy being one of 'em."

"Gramps, I think you just put us back on the right track."

"I did? How?"

"It occurred to me that we need your help." (*Zapp!*) "We'd like you to be the number-one coach for Mac and the head-shapers in the fine art of twine-tying."

"You would?"

At this, Mac cleared his throat and said, "Excuse me, Art, but I need to have a word with you. In private."

They went to the far side of the Tower and Mac said, "Listen, Art, this guy knows his job, but he's no coach. He's the main reason why nobody wants to help out."

"I'm aware of that," said Art. "That's why I am going to try to coach Gramps in how to be a good coach."

Gramps was all for the idea of being a coach to the other arrow-makers. He went straight to it.

"All right, you want a coach? Fine. Sit down and shut up and I'll tell you what to do," said Gramps. "Now, the first thing to remember about tying twine—"

"Excuse me, Gramps," said Art. "I'm glad you're willing to take up the role of coach, but it says here in this little book that the first step to being a good coach is not preaching or telling people what to do; it's asking questions."

"Really? Let me see that."

The Zapp! Wizard's Spell Book

Coaching Spell

Part I
To Be Cast by Experienced People
When Inexperienced People Are Beginning
New Tasks and Ventures.

1. Ask Questions.

2. Listen for Understanding.

3. Share Knowledge, Experience.

Coaching was very different from what Gramps had thought it was, not that he had thought much about it. He simply assumed that the way to do it was to give a lecture, watch sternly until the other person made a mistake, let it be known that the other person didn't know what he or she was doing, then bark some instructions and wait for the person to make another mistake.

But with Art Halegiver's help, Gramps learned the Coaching Spell. Though he was old and crotchety, Gramps was a quick learner and before long he was a fairly good coach.

After he learned to cast the Coaching Spell, Gramps began to ask questions and listen. Asking questions and listening let him find out what the others knew and didn't know. Rather than waiting for a mistake to reveal this, he was able to help people in advance and prevent a lot of screw-ups. And because nobody enjoys screwing up, the arrow-makers who were doing the learning liked this new approach a lot better.

Through the Coaching Spell, Gramps also discovered that it is often better to ask a question than to give the answer straight off.

"Why do you think it's so important to make that loop twice?" he would ask. Or "What would happen if we didn't use this special potion on the twine?"

When Mac or one of the others came up with the answer himself, it was HIS answer, not Gramps's. And being HIS answer, Mac would tend to keep it longer and give it a place in his mind, as he would give a prized possession a place in his home.

And when Gramps would listen for the other person to give the answer, instead of giving it himself, he was able to know if Mac and the others were just mimicking the motions or if they really understood what they were doing.

Through asking questions and listening, Gramps was able to know what the other person really needed—then he would reach into his own experience and share whatever knowledge or advice was appropriate.

As a coach, Gramps had to share a wide range of things he kept in his head. Sometimes it was information: "There are thirty-three yards of twine to a spool."

Sometimes it was knowledge: "We use this special potion to make the twine flame-proof."

Sometimes it was advice: "If you stand a little more sideways, like this, your arm won't get as tired."

Sometimes it was a story: "The reason I know to make that loop twice is because years ago the Great Sir Robert, who was before your time, came to me and said, 'Hey, kid, all the arrowheads just fell off!' Well, I took a look and … "

By the combination of asking questions and listening and sharing whatever was needed, Gramps turned Mac and the others into competent twine-tiers. As they became competent, they didn't feel stupid and they didn't mind taking their turns to do the work. Quite the opposite, in fact; by mastering a new job, Mac and the others came to feel more in control and more powerful.

Zapp!

But there were two parts to the Coaching Spell.

One part of the spell enabled Gramps to be a coach. The other part of the spell gave Mac and the other new twine-tiers the magic to get the most from the coach's advice.

The second part of the spell had similar elements as the first half, only in reverse priority.

The Zapp! Wizard's Spell Book

Coaching Spell

Part 2
To Be Cast by Those in Need of Coaching
When Beginning a New Task
or When Difficulties and Feelings
of Uncertainty Arise.

1. Share Your Needs and Problems.

2. Listen.

3. Ask Questions.

To really learn twine-tying Mac had to open up to Gramps and share things like problems and the areas in which he felt he needed to know more. Like "After I do two or three arrows, my arm gets tired." And "To do a better job, it might help if I knew why we need to make so many double loops with the twine."

Then, of course, he had to listen in order to learn.

Finally, Mac had to ask questions in order to fill in the gaps in his knowledge and understanding. "If I see the spool is nearly empty, should I start another arrow or not?" And "I don't get it; how come you use twine instead of string?"

Now, it might seem to you that there would be no need for a coaching spell, that giving and asking for advice would be an obvious and natural thing to do. But you probably live in a better place than the Magic World of Mac and his coworkers. You see, in the Land of Lamron, not knowing something, just like asking for help, was considered a sign of weakness, especially for men.

Lamronians were often afraid to admit that there were things they didn't know or couldn't do on their own. But, with the magic of the Coaching Spell, people were able to move past this fear—and in so doing, they became not weaker, but more powerful.

Zapp!

The Master Spell of Support had three spells, the second of which was the Guide-Through-Feedback Spell, and its purpose was to show people the way to better performance by giving them the right kinds of feedback at the right time.

Before he learned this spell, Gramps had always thought that feedback was saying something like "Watch what you're doing!" or "You screwed up again!"

But by reading the *Spell Book,* Art taught Gramps and the other arrow-makers that there were two kinds of feedback.

One was positive feedback; that was when, after Mac or one of the others had done something, Gramps would tell him exactly what had been done right and why.

"That looks good," Gramps would say, "because there are no loose ends to come unraveled and the wrappings are tight."

The second type of feedback was not "negative" feedback. It was instead feedback to change people's performance toward improvement.

To give the second type of feedback, Gramps had to tell Mac and the others exactly what could have been better, what to do differently, and why doing it in such a way was important.

Instead of walking over and telling Mac, "Your wrappings are too loose!" and then walking away, Gramps would say, "You need to make your wrappings tighter. Now, if you twist the twine like this as you do the wrapping, it'll end up tighter. This is real important because otherwise the arrowhead can wobble off and affect the aerodynamics."

This would give Mac enough additional knowledge

and understanding that he could guide his own performance in the right direction. Little by little, he got better and better. And as he improved, he felt a lot more energetic about his work.

Zapp!

The Zapp! Wizard's Spell Book

The Guide-Through-Feedback Spell
To help people keep going in the right direction

Positive Feedback

★ **Tell exactly what was done right.**

★ **Explain what made this action "right."**

Improvement Feedback

★ **Tell what could have been done better.**

★ **Explain your reasons why.**

★ **Provide a suggestion on how to improve.**

The third spell of the Master Spell of Support was the Spell of Encouragement. This spell injected some major magic into Tower Two, because it gave Mac and all the other arrow-makers the emotional energy to keep improving.

But Art and the others found that you had to be a little bit careful with the Encouragement Spell. It was not as easy to cast as they first thought.

If Gramps forced the magic by saying something like "Wow! That was great!" when in fact whatever Mac had done was *not* great, then the spell flopped.

Or if Gramps held off using the Encouragement Spell until everything was absolutely perfect, then the magic was very weak. Because by that time, Mac would have grown tired of waiting for the encouragement. Or might have forgotten the act for which he was being encouraged.

For the magic to be strong, the spell had to be cast in such a way that the encouragement was true.

The words had to be honest.

The feeling behind the words had to be sincere.

It was important to link encouraging words with specific actions. Just saying, "You did a good job," was weaker than saying, "You did a good job; look how you got all the potion on the twine and none on the shaft. … "

In cases of only partial success, it was important to cast the Encouragement Spell in a way that emphasized what had gone well or been done right.

And the encouragement had to be timely, spoken soon after the deed being encouraged had been done.

Yet if the words were spoken too often, they lost their power.

So the Encouragement Spell had to be used with judgment. But used at the right time and with honest

The Zapp! Wizard's Spell Book

The Encouragement Spell

People Need Encouragement to Gain Energy
for Continued Improvement

To Cast Encouragement:

Give Praise When Someone Has Done Well.

★ **Be honest.**

★ **Be specific.**

★ **Be timely.**

★ **With partial success,
   praise what went well.**

★ **Don't overdo it.**

★ **Celebrate success.**

words, this was the spell that bound together the whole Master Spell of Support.

Tower Two of Lamron Castle became a better and better place to work.

Even as Art Halegiver taught the Master Spell of Support to Gramps and the arrow-makers in Twine-Tying, he also taught its three spells to Fernanda and everyone on the Feather Floor.

Fernanda, in fact, was one of the first to sense something new and different in the air. It was a warm feeling that began to spread around the floor as the feather-gluers offered support to the shaft-turners—who, miraculously, were no longer suffering the splinter injuries that had once been epidemic, and were now happy to help out.

Shortly after casting the Encouragement Spell one day, after Art had gotten almost all of the feathers glued onto his arrows at the correct angles, Fernanda looked around and said, "What is that strange light in here?"

"I think it's yellow," said Art.

And indeed it was. With more and more support, a great golden yellow began to be seen more and more throughout the Tower, and everyone agreed it was a fine addition to the red and orange that were slowly pushing aside the usual grayness.

But this did more than just improve the atmosphere and make Tower Two a more colorful place to work. There were important and real benefits.

By supporting the shaft-turners, the feather-gluers began to get competent help and, as a result, sent more feathered shafts to Twine-Tying. And Twine-Tying, by supporting the head-shapers, got help that enabled Gramps and his coworkers to move more finished arrows each day to the top of the Tower for the magic to be added.

Bucket by bucket and bundle by bundle, the huge backlog of arrowheads and arrow shafts began to go down. And as the buckets and bundles went down, the number of finished Magic Arrows going to the knights fighting the dragons began—finally!—to go up.

The Boss watched the numbers climb day by day: 106, 109, 119, 136, 144, 158, 182 finished Magic Arrows!

Now the Boss began to jump up and down with excitement. Now the Boss really began to see and believe the true power of Zapp!

So now she went down to Art Halegiver and borrowed *The Zapp! Wizard Spell Book.*

Back in her office, she was flipping through its pages when the latest floating-eyeball report came in. She glanced at the report and gasped.

With a sigh of disappointment, she closed the *Spell Book* and returned it to Art.

"Wow," said Art as the Boss handed back the *Spell Book,* "you must be a fast reader."

"I didn't bother reading it all the way through," said the Boss.

"Why not?"

"This Zapp! magic is strong, but it's only temporary," said the Boss.

Art looked around at the red, orange, and yellow colors and the lightning bolts flashing back and forth between people around him and said, "It still looks pretty strong to me."

"Well, take a look at these," said the Boss. And she showed him the latest report: Only a hundred and ten Magic Arrows had been completed the day before.

"Gee, that's quite a drop," said Art. "Of course, I can show you why it happened."

"You can?"

"Sure. Come with me."

He took the Boss up the steps to the Feather Floor. When Art opened the door, the Boss stepped back, expecting those piled-up bundles of arrow shafts to spill down the steps. But nothing fell out the door. There were no piles left.

"It's the same in Twine-Tying," said Art. "Don't you see? The problem is not with the magic. We've eliminated the backlog."

Then Art showed the Boss mathematically what was going on:

In the Shaftshop, there were three shaft-turners who were turning out about twenty-five arrow shafts a day, plus Art himself, who had doubled his regular output and was turning out fifty shafts. That made a grand total average of one hundred twenty-five arrow shafts.

In the arrowhead area, there were four head-shapers, who were making about twenty arrowheads a day, plus Mac, who had increased his output by 80 percent and so was hammering out about thirty-six heads a day. That meant about a hundred sixteen arrowheads on a typical day.

"And of course," said Art, "if the shaft-turners and head-shapers are helping out the feather-gluers and twine-tiers, the numbers will be less."

This was a bit tricky for the Boss to understand.

"You see," said Art, "because we have to depend on one another, the maximum output for the whole Tower is going to be the smallest output of any of the five groups. So if the shaft-turners turn out a hundred twenty-five shafts, but the head-shapers only put out a hundred sixteen heads, then the whole Tower can finish a maximum of only a hundred sixteen Magic Arrows."

"Aha," said the Boss. "It's kind of like a chain only being as strong as its weakest link."

"Kind of."

"Yesterday we didn't even make a hundred and sixteen," said the Boss.

"I guess one of the groups had a bad day," said Art. "When one group has a bad day, it's going to lower the output for the whole Tower."

Now, this is when the Boss did a great thing. In the face of this depressing revelation, she could have said to herself, "Well, what the heck. For the moment at least,

I've got the ten percent improvement the dukes were asking for. That's good enough."

But the Boss didn't say that to herself. She instead said to Art Halegiver, "Give me that *Zapp! Wizard Spell Book* again."

The Boss took the book back to her office and began flipping through it once more, hoping something would pop out at her and give her a clue as to what she should do.

She was reading over the Three Keys Spell, when suddenly the page began to glow. And in big golden letters, some new words appeared, as if intended for her eyes only, below the main part of the spell.

For quite a while, the Boss thought about what these new words might mean. Then she sent word that she wanted to meet with Art, Mac, and Wendy.

They met in a spare room of the Tower, which until recently had been filled with spare arrow parts.

"You three have fairly well established yourselves as the leaders of the whole improvement effort brought about by Zapp!," said the Boss. "So I wanted to ask you, do you really think that a hundred ten or a hundred sixteen Magic Arrows a day or thereabouts is the best we can do?"

"Heck, no," said Mac. "Sir Fred said that the knights needed double the Magic Arrows we were producing—and I really think we can meet that goal."

"Me, too," said Art. "I've doubled my output, but

none of the other shaft-turners have improved very much, even though they're as capable as I am. I don't see why all four of us can't average fifty shafts a day."

"Same with the head-shapers," said Mac.

"Same with the wand-wavers," said Wendy, "and as for the twine-tiers and feather-gluers, they haven't even started the kinds of improvements that we've made in our own processes."

"All right," said the Boss. "What can I do to help you and the other arrow-makers continue to improve?"

The three arrow-makers could feel a wave of energy enter themselves.

They talked openly about what kind of help they needed from the Boss, and they came up with three things.

They asked for time to solve problems.

They asked the Boss to share more information with them.

And they asked her to help them get whatever tools and materials they needed to bring about their improvements.

"You've got 'em," said the Boss.

They agreed on how and when they would check back with the Boss for guidance and to report on progress. Then the Boss left the room. And she left something behind.

She left a tremendous Zapp! for the three arrow-makers.

In the past, when the Boss left the room, she almost always took the problem with her. She might ask for opinions from the arrow-makers, but she always carried the responsibility for solving the problem with her out the door.

Not this time. This time she left the problem—and the challenge—of doubling Tower Two's Magic Arrow output with the three arrow-makers.

Zapp!

When the Boss got back to her office, she found on her desk a bright platinum key.

No one, least of all herself, knew where the platinum key had come from. But it seemed to be from the same family as the bronze, silver, and gold keys the Boss had already collected using the Three Keys Spell.

On the side of the platinum key were the words ...

Offer Help Without Taking Responsibility for Action

These were the same words that had appeared before the Boss's eyes below the Three Keys Spell.

She got out the small wooden chest that the arrow-makers had given her some time before, and fitted each of her four keys into the four locks.

The Boss turned the keys ... and the chest opened.

First to come out of the chest was a bright ball of light that drifted out of the Boss's office, quickly expanded, joined with the other lights in the Tower, and greatly increased their brilliance. From that day forward, the power of all Zapp! spells cast in Tower Two was multiplied several times over.

The Boss checked the chest to see if it contained anything else. It did. Inside was another spell book, this one entitled: *The Zapp! Wizard's Spell Book For Bosses*.

Well, the Boss settled back and opened her very own spell book, which had all of the spells that the arrow-makers were learning, plus a number of others that could only be cast by bosses.

These spells gave her some powerful magic of her own that allowed her to delegate authority (and still know what was going on), set clear goals, and other neat tricks.

It took many moons, but with time and practice, the Boss learned these spells. Much to the satisfaction of Art, Mac, and Wendy, the Boss became more than just a boss.

She became a leader.

10

Meanwhile, back in the spare room, Wendy, Mac, and Art were in a state of amazement.

"Wow, the Boss really trusts us!" said Wendy.

"Yeah, I can hardly believe how much," said Mac.

"A few moons ago," said Art, "I never would have expected it."

Then the realization of what they had to do hit them.

"Wow, we've got a lot of things to get done!" said Wendy.

"Yeah, I can hardly believe how much," said Mac.

"A few moons from now," said Art, "we've got to have done what we said we'd have done!"

So they got down to work.

The first thing they did, because of their past mistakes, was to make sure that everybody in Tower Two knew what was important and what the goal was: two hundred arrows a day.

Then they made sure that everybody knew the score. Toward the end of the day, Wendy would write down the total number of arrows finished and post it by the door so that all the arrow-makers could see it both when they left and when they came in the next morning.

She also filled in the numbers on a large chart next to the daily total, and day by day, the arrow-makers began to see their performance—good or bad.

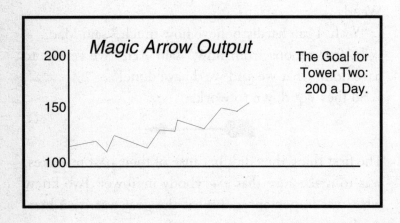

Today's
Magic Arrow
Output:

148!

Magic Arrow Output

200

150

100

The Goal for
Tower Two:
200 a Day.

Wendy, Mac, and Art met with their fellow arrow-makers individually to help each of them set personal goals for their work that would fit with the overall goal for the whole Tower. And they encouraged all the arrow-makers to measure their personal progress daily.

Not all the arrow-makers had the same goal, of course, because they had different jobs and also because some people were less experienced than others. Often, the arrow-makers would have to set smaller goals that they would have meet in order to accomplish a larger one. But in time, if everyone could meet their goals, then the overall goal could be achieved.

Along the way Art, Mac, Wendy, and the other arrow-makers used all the Zapp! Magic they knew.

They cast the Master Spell of Support, for instance, so that the other arrow-makers would be encouraged by this progress and be motivated to overcome obstacles.

Zapp!

Fairly soon, using the ACTION Spell and others, Tower Two began to see a lot of little improvements from top to bottom.

Fernanda discovered that she spent a lot of time during the day flattening the feathers that would be glued onto the arrow shafts. So she and her coworkers figured out a way to flatten the feathers overnight by piling heavy blocks on top of them. Minutes not spent flattening meant more minutes for gluing.

Art, Mac, and Wendy shared their improvement ideas with their coworkers. They used the Three Keys Spell to safeguard against the danger that people would feel somehow inadequate or jealous for not thinking of these ideas themselves. And they allowed the other arrow-makers to put their own individual stamps on these ideas. By playing with the original idea, the arrow-makers could often improve upon one another's improvements.

FROM THE WORKBENCH OF: **ART HALEGIVER**

Tower Two Lamron Castle

When Working on Improvements . . .

TWO HEADS ARE BETTER THAN ONE AND MANY HEADS ARE BETTER THAN TWO!

Sometimes a fresh point of view made a big difference. Gramps found that, contrary to general opinion, he did not know everything about tying arrowheads to shafts with twine. Because of his intimate knowledge of arrowheads, Mac (while invoking the Three Keys Spell) was able to point out that a simple twist here and a loop there would actually hold the arrowhead tighter while eliminating several knots that were tricky and time-consuming to tie.

Based on this, Gramps and the twine-tiers were able to save several minutes on every arrow. Yet this never would have happened if Mac had not done his stint in Twine-Tying with the other head-shapers.

It worked the other way, too. With the help of the Master Spell of Support, all of the different work groups began to learn different jobs in the Tower. That way if someone caught Lamronian flu and didn't show up for work, or if one of the groups had a problem and fell behind, the other groups could lend support by sending an arrow-maker or two to help.

Well, one morning the woodcutter was late getting to the castle and the shaft-turners ran out of stock and fell behind. So Fernanda came down that afternoon and helped in the Shaftshop.

"Say, Art, tell me something," she said. "Why do you shaft-turners take the time to tie all the arrow shafts in neat little bundles?"

"Well, we always thought you wanted them that way," said Art.

"No, it doesn't matter to us if they're in neat little bundles," said Fernanda. "To tell you the truth, it's trouble for everybody, because you have to count out a dozen shafts and tie them in a bundle, and then upstairs, we feather-gluers just have to *un*tie them."

They quickly figured out that at least half an hour out of every day went into bundling the shafts, a step that really wasn't necessary and that they just automatically performed, unaware of how much time it really robbed from them each day. Now, half an hour might not sound like such a big deal, but if you add up that half hour day by day by day, you've got quite a chunk of time.

So they cast the ACTION Spell and tried some alternatives. Instead of tying the shafts in bundles, they tried carrying the arrow shafts in buckets like the ones the head-shapers used (too small). Then they tried wooden barrels (too heavy). Finally, one of the shaft-turners brought from home a long, narrow wicker basket that was lightweight and just about the right size.

They had a few more of these baskets made up in town for a couple pieces of gold from the Boss's budget. From then on, as the shaft-turners finished their shafts, they put them in these baskets, and when a basket was full, someone carried it to the Feather Floor. It was a simple solution that gave them the time to turn out six to eight extra shafts every day.

These little improvements began to add up and multiply. Before long, the number of arrows reaching Wendy and the other wand-wavers went up and up and up—so much so that the wand-wavers almost never had time on their hands. They, too, had to become more inventive in how they did their magic work.

Sometimes, even the wand-wavers needed temporary help at the top of the Tower from the other arrow-makers. Though one had to be licensed to wave a wand, there were setup procedures that anyone could perform with the right training.

When the numbers went up on the wall at the bottom of Tower Two at the end of the day, they did not lie: 116, 121, 119, 125, 127, 124, 131.

The numbers did not always go up. There were bad days, there were good days. And there were periods when the average didn't change.

Now, the Boss was doing everything she said she would. She was allowing the arrow-makers time to talk and use the ACTION Spell. She gave them gold for things like the baskets and special tools. She was sharing more information with them. Best of all, though, when she saw that the arrow-makers were stalled or having trouble, she would step in and offer help.

The Boss went to Art, Mac, and Wendy one day and said, "I've been noticing that the count of finished arrows has been dropping a little bit."

"We've been noticing it, too," said Mac.

"Where do you think the trouble is?"

"We're not sure," said Art, "but one thing I've noticed is we're spending a lot of time in meetings and in talking to one another. And while we appreciate your allowing us the time, it seems that we don't get very much accomplished in these meetings."

"Yes, I've been worried about the same thing," said the Boss. "Tell you what, I'm an old hand at meetings. Why don't I sit in on a couple of yours and see if I can spot why these meetings are taking so much time."

"Good idea," said Art.

The next afternoon, the shaft-turners got together and the Boss sat in. Art Halegiver was running the meeting, and he opened by saying a few words to cast the Three Keys Spell.

"We can all be proud we're working so well together"—*Zapp!*—"and I know we all want our progress to continue," said Art. "So I'd like your help on an important issue."

Zapp!

"We need to decide if we should increase our standing order of shaft stock from the woodcutters," Art continued, "and decide whether two deliveries a week is still enough."

"That's a good thing to talk about," said Jorge, one of Art's fellow shaft-turners. "I know that I have run out of stock several times in the past few weeks." And he went on to describe in some detail the irritation he felt when this occurred.

Art listened and responded with empathy. "So you feel frustrated and angry when you run out of stock."

"Yes, I do," said Jorge.

Zapp!

"By the way," said Louise, another shaft-turner, "I think we need to coordinate better who sweeps up the wood shavings at the end of the day."

Art listened and appropriately empathized with her feeling that she had done more than her share of the sweeping.

Zapp!

"Yeah," said Joe, "but we also have to consider what to do with those wood shavings."

And on and on. After half an hour, though, it was time to go back to work.

"Wait a minute!" said Art. "We didn't decide how much stock to order!"

"Well," said Louise, "let's get together same time tomorrow and we'll work on it then."

When the other shaft-turners had gone back to work, Art said to the Boss, "You see? I was using the Three Keys Spell, but we didn't get done what we needed to. Just as I was trying to get some numbers from everybody to place an order, all of a sudden we're off on wood shavings and who should sweep the floor! Where did I go wrong?"

"So far as the Three Keys Spell, I don't think you did anything wrong," said the Boss. "Why don't we recheck the *Spell Book* and see if it says anything to help us."

Art got out *The Zapp! Wizard's Spell Book* and went through it with the Boss. On the back side of the Three Keys Spell, sure enough, there was a long page of small print containing warnings and disclaimers that Art had skipped because it looked like dull reading, which it was. Basically it said this:

Warning. People in an organization have two kinds of needs. They have personal needs. That is, people need to think of themselves as being valued. They need to have their feelings respected. And each person needs to be considered an

important member of the group.

However, people in an organization also have practical needs. Practical needs are things like getting the right information, having a clear direction set, having the proper tools, meeting schedules, and so on.

Then the book said, "The Three Keys Spell primarily addresses personal needs. For Zapp! Magic that addresses practical needs, see the ACTION Spell."

"See," said the Boss, "in the meeting, you were doing fine with the personal needs, but the reason you called the meeting was to work out a practical problem."

"You know, I thought about casting the ACTION Spell," said Art, "but it didn't seem to apply. We weren't really dealing with a problem. We were just meeting to collect information and make a decision."

"Let's check the ACTION Spell anyway."

They did. And down at the bottom of the page, in small type, was a message that read:

For general discussions and meetings, try the Inter-ACTION variation of the ACTION Spell. To read this spell, snap your fingers three times and say the words:

"Let's get practical."

Art and the Boss faced each other, snapped their fingers, and said the words in unison—and there was a low roll of thunder. The words of the ACTION Spell began to change and move around on the *Spell Book* page. When the thunder stopped, the words settled

The Zapp! Wizard's Spell Book

The InterACTION Spell

Based on the same magic as the ACTION Spell, the InterACTION Spell can be cast in all kinds of practical discussions, whether one-on-one, or in group meetings with many people. It will work in any practical situation in which participants need to stay on track and arrive at a decision with others.

To Cast:

1. **Open with what is to be accomplished and why it is important.**

2. **Clarify the details.**

3. **Develop ideas.**

4. **Agree on actions.**

5. **Close with review of decisions and set appropriate follow-up.**

into new places, and the ACTION Spell had become the InterACTION Spell.

So in the meeting the next day Art cast the InterACTION Spell.

He opened with what the purpose of the meeting was and why it was important.

Then he clarified the details by getting the shaft-turners to give him numbers regarding the shaft stock currently in supply and what their future needs were likely to be.

Next, the shaft-turners exchanged ideas on whether they needed to increase the stock order and how often the stock should be delivered.

They agreed on actions: Jorge would ask the wood-cutters to increase deliveries from twice a week to three times a week, and Louise would check the stock supply twice a day to determine if there would be enough to last until the next delivery.

Finally, Art checked to be sure everyone understood what was going to happen by reviewing the decision and the reason for it. And he got them to agree on the con-ditions under which they would discuss this issue again—Louise would alert them if a run-out was likely or if they had excess stock piling up.

Each time someone brought up a new topic that would take the meeting off on a tangent, Art would carefully redirect the conversation back to the part of the InterACTION Spell they were currently dealing with. The spell gave them a structure, so that they knew where they were at all times in the discussion, and what they had to cover before moving on to a new topic.

Art taught the InterACTION Spell to the rest of the arrow-makers, as well as the Boss. And with this spell, they had a way not just to solve problems, but to make all their discussions more productive.

Zapp!

Before long, there was another new color in the Tower: green. It was a very nice green, a shade that had never, ever been seen within the castle until now.

One little idea …
One little improvement …
One little Zapp! at a time.

That was how the arrow-makers transformed Tower Two from a workplace of fog and dullness into a bright place with a sense that anything was possible.

They changed it from a place where everybody dutifully came to work and did what was required into a tower where everybody wanted to work and give their very best.

And with the aid of Dave's spells and the Boss's support, they did it pretty much on their own.

Every time the arrow count went up, there was a cheer as the arrow-makers left for the day. Just as important, every time the arrow count dropped or stayed the same for a long period, everybody was concerned.

Once they knew the goal, knew the score, and knew they had the Zapp! to affect the outcome, everybody cared.

The numbers slowly climbed.

The chart next to the daily total showed the progress: 133, 131, 129, 133, 136.

Then: 137, 144, 149, 151, 148.

Then: 142, 150, 154, 149, 160.

Then: 161, 162, 160, 168, 172.

Then numbers stayed in the 170-to-180 range for quite a while.

Mac, Wendy, and Art met with the Boss, and Art said, "Boss, in all honesty, we need more hands. I'm sure that in time we could find the improvements to reach two hundred arrows a day. But to do it anytime soon, especially before the Dragon Moon, we've got to have more people helping to make arrows."

"I know you're sincere," said the Boss, "but with the King's edict prohibiting hiring more castle workers, what am I to do?"

"We've thought about this," said Wendy, "and we've come up with an idea."

There were a number of people in the castle who did work that was kind of important, but didn't directly contribute to making Magic Arrows or fighting drag-ons. Why not "borrow" some of these people, at least temporarily, to help in Tower Two? This way, the castle would not be paying much, if anything, extra in payroll gold, but Tower Two could get these people to help reach the goal.

The Boss thought this was a worthy idea. She helped the three arrow-makers present this idea to the Duke of Arrows, and the duke said, "Try it."

In a few days, the Boss was able to round up a stable-hand, a knight's squire, a couple of castle criers, and even a duke's assistant. The arrow-makers cast the Master Spell of Support and not only made the new people feel at home, but also made them productive. And a week or so later, the finished Magic Arrow count had risen to the 190s.

Then came the afternoon—it happened to be a Friday—when Art Halegiver was wrapping up for the day and he tallied his numbers and discovered he had personally turned out seventy-one arrow shafts. He looked around at the other shaft-turners' measurements and saw a 58, a 63, a 49 ... and he realized that they were well past two hundred shafts for the day.

He mentioned this fact to the others, and there was a buzz of excitement.

He went upstairs to the Feather Floor, talked to Fernanda, and learned that the feather-gluers had not done quite as well, but still had feathered two hundred and nineteen shafts that day.

By the time Art and the other arrow-makers got to Twine-Tying, Gramps was dancing around with the two hundred and first finished arrow.

"Well, don't just dance with it!" said Art. "Take it up to the Magic Room."

Art went over to the arrowhead area and got Mac. Together they went to the top of the Tower, where Wendy and the wand-wavers were waving wands like crazy.

The other arrow-makers counted as Wendy and her coworkers finished: "One hundred ninety-seven ... one hundred ninety-eight ... one hundred ninety-nine ... two-hundred!"

"We've done it!" shouted Art Halegiver.

It was true. For the first time in the history of Tower Two, the arrow-makers had made two hundred arrows in a single day. The arrow-makers of Tower Two had finally accomplished what their customers, the knights, had asked. They had doubled the number of Magic Arrows they made.

11

All of the arrow-makers of Tower Two celebrated. There were handshakes and pats on the back and smiles all around. The Boss herself went around and congratulated each individual arrow-maker and said, "Thanks for helping. Thanks for being part of this."

Then they went home for the weekend.

When they came back on Monday morning, the entire Tower lit up in shades of the new colors and everybody set to work making more Magic Arrows. By midweek, it was clear that Friday's performance had been no fluke; they were really turning out the arrows now.

A few days later, before work started, the Boss came around and said, "Excuse me, everybody, but we all need to talk. It seems there is a little problem."

Little problem? What could that be? All the arrow-makers of Tower Two gathered in the courtyard.

"We're going to have to change the goal," said the Boss.

Everybody groaned.

"What do the knights want now?" asked Mac. "Do they want us to *quadruple* the number of arrows?"

The Boss began to blush. "No, the Duke of Arrows asked to see me yesterday. I thought he was going to compliment us on the fact that Tower Two had met and far exceeded its ten percent improvement well in advance of the Dragon Moon. Instead, the Duke of Accounting was there as well. It seems they are quite alarmed at the castle's skyrocketing expenses on Magic Arrows."

"Of course the costs are going to go up," Wendy pointed out. "We've doubled the number of arrows we're making, so we've doubled the materials we need to buy!"

"Yes, and that's why they are alarmed," said the Boss. "You see, this castle is not in the Magic Arrow business. This castle is in the dragon-fighting business. If it takes one Magic Arrow to subdue the dragon or a hundred Magic Arrows, the castle makes the same amount of gold."

"Aha," said all the arrow-makers.

"And," the Boss continued, "with the gold reserves in the Treasure Room being very low … well, let's just say the situation is not good."

"But Sir Fred said we should double the number of arrows we made!" protested Art.

"Sir Fred was off the mark," said the Boss.

"Why would he tell us that?"

"I don't know," said the Boss.

"Well, I think we ought to go see Sir Fred and the knights and ask them what the real story is," said Mac.

"I think that is a great idea," said the Boss. "In fact, I will go along with you."

Mac, Art, Wendy, and the Boss went over to the Knights' Keep, where they found Sir Fred in a rather agitated state. He was bent over his desk as his squire attempted to remove one of Tower Two's Magic Arrows, which was protruding from his butt.

"Gee, what happened, Sir Fred?" asked Wendy. "Did you have an accident?"

"Accident?" roared Sir Fred. "This was no accident! This is the price of bad quality!"

It took Sir Fred a while to calm down enough to talk, but it seemed Sir Fred had gone out that morning to fight one of the big Mother Dragons. When he shot his Magic Arrow, it went up in the air, made a big loop, missed the Mother Dragon completely, came around, and hit Sir Fred in the backside.

Luckily, he was wearing armored underwear.

"The so-called Magic Arrows you people are turning out today aren't worth the feathers glued to them!" said Sir Fred, and he bellowed further that he had fired a full quiver of arrows, yet it took three direct hits to make the Mother Dragon disappear.

"Then why did you tell us to double the number we were making?" asked the Boss.

"Because when I told you to double the arrows, I thought that you would make more *good* ones! It seems that the opposite is the case!"

Mac, Art, Wendy, and the Boss all began to turn gray. They slowly returned to Tower Two, which already had lost much of the nice natural color it had been gaining in recent weeks. All the shades were there, but they looked washed out now.

When lunchtime came, Art joined Mac and Wendy at the usual courtyard table and saw that they both looked depressed.

"Everything we've done was just a waste!" complained Wendy.

"No, I disagree," said Art. "What we accomplished was not a waste."

"Why not?"

"Because in the past few moons we've learned *how to improve*. And we've learned a lot about ourselves. That's worth a bunch more than just knowing how to make more arrows."

"Yeah, that's true," Mac agreed. "We made a mistake because other people didn't think about what they were asking us to do—and maybe it's partly our fault, maybe we should have questioned them more. But, you know, when we crossed that two hundred mark, we proved what we can do."

"That's right. We showed that when we work together toward a common goal, we can reach it," said Art. "And now that we know how to work together, we can set a new goal and attack the real problems."

"Okay, but I don't even know where to begin," said Wendy.

"The place to begin, it seems to me, is the same as it

was the first time," said Art. "We want to start with a goal and measurements. Only this time we need a goal for Tower Two that fits the overall mission of the castle."

FROM THE WORKBENCH OF: **ART HALEGIVER**

Tower Two Lamron Castle

Quantity is only one aspect of being productive.

FROM THE WORKBENCH OF: **ART HALEGIVER**

Tower Two Lamron Castle

We've got to be sure the goal we seek is a goal worth pursuing.

In the next few days, Mac, Art, and Wendy got together with their customers, the knights and with the Boss; then together with the other arrow-makers of Tower Two they set a new goal.

Instead of "Double the number of arrows produced daily from one hundred to two hundred," they all decided this might be better:

**The New Goal
for Tower Two:**

*Provide Magic Arrows that meet
100 percent of our knights'
requirements for quality and quantity
100 percent of the time.*

This time, to be absolutely sure that this goal was one that would really support the castle's overall mission, they wrote it down, showed it to the Boss, to Sir Fred and the knights, and to the Duke of Arrows, and got them all to agree that this was a worthy and noble goal that would help ensure the long-term prosperity of the castle.

Well, the Duke of Arrows, partly because he wanted to be sure that *he* was right in giving his approval to the goal and partly because he was so impressed with the arrow-makers' initiative, went and showed this goal to the King.

And when the King saw this and heard the duke's story of how the arrow-makers of Tower Two had set a goal for themselves and worked together to reach it and were now setting a new goal in response to new information and new needs, the King rejoiced.

"Finally!" said the King, clasped hands in the air. "Finally, we have some hope!"

But how to reach the new goal, that was the question. To be successful, Mac, Art, and Wendy had to get everyone in Tower Two thinking in a new and different way.

"Let's get people together," suggested Mac, "and let's get working on some improvements that will get us to reach the new goal."

And that was what they did. They got everyone together. They cast the ACTION Spell. And afterward, everyone agreed that the meeting had been very productive.

Which it would have been, except for one thing.

They agreed on a course of action that was completely off-target.

Soon after the meeting, the arrow-makers all pitched in and made some banners with slogans saying things like "Quality Is Important!" and "Don't Make Any Mistakes!" and the ever-popular "Do It Right the First Time!"

It was not that there was anything wrong with these slogans, and the banners looked great hung here and there around the Tower—but that was *all* they did.

Needless to say, quality did not improve.

Word continued to filter back from the knights that the arrows were still missing the dragons' hearts and that they, the knights, were no happier about it than before.

"Now what?" asked Art.

"I think we should get everybody to be aware," said Wendy, "that slogans aren't enough. We need to pin down exactly *how* we're going to improve quality."

So they held another meeting, they cast the ACTION Spell, and the discussion went round and round a single question:

"What is quality?" asked Art.

"Well," said Fernanda, "I think quality means having the same color feathers on each arrow."

"Well," said Mac, "I think quality is having arrowheads that are bright and polished."

"Well," said Wendy, "I think quality is that 'extra something'—like a big red ribbon around each shaft."

Since they could not rule out any of these things as being "quality," they agreed to do all of them. For the next week, they worked very hard at keeping the feathers on each arrow the same color, and making sure the arrows were bright and polished. And just before the arrows were delivered to the knights, Wendy and several other arrow-makers spent time tying big, curly red ribbons around each shaft.

However, the knights were not very appreciative of these efforts.

When Art went to ask them how they liked these quality improvements, the knights pretty much said the same thing: "It's great that the arrows look nicer now, but your quality still stinks. And those red ribbons are a hazard! The arrows get all tangled up and the dragons can see that red color miles away! Then we can't sneak up on them! The first thing we do when we get new arrows is rip off the ribbon and throw it in the trash!"

So then Art came up with an idea. He said to Mac and Wendy, "Look, we can't tell the knights what quality is! They're our customers, remember? They have to tell us!"

"What are you suggesting?" asked Wendy.

"Let's go to the knights and get them to define what quality means."

They did this. They cast the InterACTION Spell, and they found that there were three things that the knights valued in a quality Magic Arrow:

1. The arrow had to fly straight and
hit the target.

2. The arrow had to penetrate the
dragons' thick scales.

3. No duds—the magic had to work
first time, every time.

Everything else—the polished and shiny arrowheads, the matching colors of feathers, etc.—was secondary to those three criteria.

FROM THE WORKBENCH OF: **ART HALEGIVER**

Tower Two Lamron Castle

To Improve Quality Is to Improve What the Customer Values.

"Terrific," said Wendy. "Now we know what we're shooting for. But how are we to know if we're really improving quality?"

"The same way we could tell if we were improving quantity," said Art. "We measure it."

"Measure it?" asked Wendy. "How can you measure quality?"

"We can measure it because the knights have told us the specific things that are essential to a quality Magic Arrow: A quality arrow flys right, penetrates the dragon's scales, and makes the dragon vanish every time."

"So?"

"So now we need to figure out what makes a perfect Magic Arrow," said Art. "We need to ask, What characteristics cause the Magic Arrow to do its job right? And what deviations from perfection allow a Magic Arrow to fail? Once we know those things, then we set up measurements and start to improve."

"Right," said Wendy with sarcasm. "Sounds real easy."

"I'm not saying it's easy," said Art, "but that's what we have to do."

"Okay, where do we start?" she asked.

"The ACTION Spell," said Mac. "We need the ACTION Spell to get through this."

The first part of the ACTION Spell was to assess the situation and define the problem. So over several days, some of the arrow-makers went out with the knights when they battled the dragons. The arrow-makers stayed back, out of harm's way, and simply counted how many of the Magic Arrows did what they were supposed to do.

When all the data were tallied, this was the result:

For every one hundred Magic Arrows, only eighty flew straight; twenty did not fly right and therefore missed the dragon completely.

Of the remaining eighty arrows that hit the dragon, only sixty-four penetrated the dragon's scales; sixteen bounced off and landed on the ground.

Of the sixty-four arrows that went to the heart, only fifty-one sent the dragon back to a parallel dimension; thirteen were duds.

Therefore, of one hundred Magic Arrows, only fifty-one worked perfectly and did everything that a Magic Arrow was supposed to do; forty-nine failed for one reason or another.

"Now I can see why Sir Fred wanted us to make twice as many arrows," said Mac. "With only half of all the arrows doing what they were supposed to do ... Well, his reasoning was off the mark, but I can see why he asked for what he did."

"But what caused the forty-nine to fail?" asked Art.

"For that," said Mac, "I guess we have to get into all the technicalities."

12

hen I have an idea," said Wendy. "Let's ask the wizards over in the R&D Dungeon. They're in charge of how Magic Arrows are designed. If anyone would know, they would."

They went across the courtyard and over to the R&D Dungeon, where most of the techno-wizards worked. There, the Grand Techno-Wizard (or GTW) granted them an audience, and after they explained what they wanted, the GTW took them into a large room lined with file cabinets. The GTW opened a drawer, pulled out a big, round scroll, blew the dust off, and handed it to them.

"What's this?"

"It's a quality study we conducted a couple of eons ago. It'll tell you all the reasons why Magic Arrows don't fly straight."

"Well, if you wizards know the causes of our quality problems, why haven't you done anything?"

"That's not our department," said the GTW. "Our orders from the King were simply to conduct the study, not to do anything with the results."

Indeed, this happened frequently around the castle.

There was lots of information and lots of ideas, but nobody ever did anything with them.

Mac, Art, and Wendy took the heavy, thick scroll back to Tower Two and read through it. Of course, it was written in Wizardese, the technical language spoken only by wizards to their fellow wizards, but with a little bit of deciphering, the three arrow-makers figured out what it said.

One of the more intriguing parts of the scroll was this:

It seemed that a long time ago, an Unknown Somebody had decided, "Hey, four outta five ain't bad." That is, in each case, there was 80 percent success in each and every function required of a Magic Arrow.

That is, 80 percent (four out of five) arrow shafts flew straight when shot from a bow.

And 80 percent of the arrowheads were sharp enough and had just the right weight to penetrate the dragon's scales and hit the heart. But that 80 percent wasn't necessarily fastened to the 80 percent of the arrow shafts that flew straight. Some of the "good" arrowheads were fastened to shafts that missed the target.

Same thing with the magic: Eighty percent of the time the magic worked. But the working 80 percent was not always carried to the dragon's heart by a good shaft with a good head. If the shaft and the arrowhead failed, the magic never got a chance to work.

So, as the wizards put it, there were dependencies among the different functions. If one function didn't work, the entire arrow was a wasted arrow, and while the odds of one function being good were 80:20, the odds of any single arrow having all three functions work correctly in sequence were much, much lower.

"Well," said Art, "that explains why the failures in the field are so high."

As the three arrow-makers read further, they discovered that the wizards had also identified the causes of Magic Arrow failures.

"It says here," said Wendy, who understood Wizardese better than the others, "that eighty percent of all Magic Arrow failures, regardless of which function failed, have one underlying cause."

"Really?" asked Art. "What's that?"

"Gremlins."

"Gremlins? What are gremlins?"

"Why, gremlins are little ugly critters that scoot in when you're not looking and mess things up," said Mac.

"But I've never seen gremlins around here," said Art.

"Well, of course you wouldn't," said Wendy. "It says in this scroll that the gremlins are invisible."

"Invisible? How can they be invisible?"

"Because the gremlins are from the same parallel dimension as the dragons," said Wendy.

"You mean they can sneak around in this parallel dimension and we can't see them, but they can see us?"

"Yes. It is even suspected that they are the allies of the dragons, messing us up so that the dragons can have their fun."

"Well, what can we do to fight invisible creatures from another dimension?" asked Art.

"We have to make Tower Two gremlin-proof," said Wendy.

This is how the arrow-makers of Tower Two fought the invisible gremlins who were messing up their quality.

The arrow-makers first figured out exactly what was the best Magic Arrow they could make with the people and tools they had at hand. This was an imaginary Magic Arrow, one they would always strive to create but would never realize due to gremlins and other realities.

Now, they gave this imaginary Magic Arrow exact characteristics. It should be so long; it should weigh so much; the feathers had to be at such and such an angle, and so on. But they were not as exact with some characteristics as they were with others.

Like the length of the arrows was important, but it wasn't *that* important. It was nice for the sake of appearances if the arrows were the same length. But if the arrow was a tiny bit longer or a tiny bit shorter, it didn't really matter.

It was the same with the color of the feathers. It was nice if the feathers matched, but this was not something the knights cared a lot about, because a dragon was no more or no less likely to disappear if the feathers were green or yellow or whatever.

But the angle of the feathers was very important. If the gremlins messed up the angle of the feathers just a little bit, the arrow would not fly right. Same with the straightness of the shaft, the hardness and sharpness of the arrowheads, and the reliability of the magic. All of those were extremely important. Because all of those would influence the values that the knights considered most important. For those, the arrow-makers were very, very exact.

FROM THE WORKBENCH OF: **ART HALEGIVER**

Tower Two Lamron Castle

First Improve What's Most Important to the Customer.

By now, they had learned the hard lesson that they could not invent this information on their own. To create the perfect imaginary Magic Arrow, they had to consult with others—the wizards, the knights, and the Boss all being key people to guide them.

Once they had the perfect arrow, they set up measurements and tests. Then they began to check how close the real arrows were to the perfect imaginary Magic Arrow.

And by these measurements and tests, they could tell where the gremlins had been making mischief.

For instance, Art kept very careful records of the straightness of the arrow shafts he was turning. When the numbers began to drift one way or another, and the deviation from the imaginary perfect Magic Arrow became significant, then he would know that the invisible gremlins had been fooling around with his lathe. He would stop and reset the equipment—and the gremlins would move on to bother someone else.

He and Fernanda worked together to gremlin-proof the angle of the feathers by making a simple tool that would always set the feathers correctly.

Whenever Mac finished an arrowhead, he would see if it would slice like a razor through a sheet of paper. If it did not, then Mac knew that the gremlins had been messing with his sharpener. Over time, he found little ways to gremlin-proof the sharpener so that it hardly ever went out of adjustment.

Wendy worked with the wizards to create a special ring. By passing one's hand over a quiver of arrows, the ring bearer could check whether the magic had "taken" and the arrows were potent. If one or more of the arrows did not glow brightly in the presence of the ring, Wendy or one of the other wand-wavers would remove it from the quiver. Then they would try to figure out what the gremlins had done to make the magic fail.

After they had gremlin-proofed one part of the process, starting with whatever was most important, each arrow-maker would then focus on whatever was the next most important. And on and on.

FROM THE WORKBENCH OF: **ART HALEGIVER**

Tower Two Lamron Castle

With Quality Improvement Never Be Satisified.

The time of the Dragon Moon arrived.

The knights were constantly being called to battle. From all over Lamron, the horns summoning help were sounding.

One day, at the very height of the Dragon Moon, Sir Fred galloped out alone ready for a fight, but when he got to the scene he became numb with fear.

It had been a one-trumpet alarm, but facing him were four dragons. They had trapped some travelers who were on the highway, away from shelter, and the dragons were getting ready to have a big picnic.

Sir Fred checked his quiver. There were four dragons, but he had brought with him a dozen Magic Arrows. He spurred his mount and galloped to save the people who were trapped.

But as he rode in, he sensed something to his left, and

when he turned to look there were four more dragons, making eight in all. This was not good.

He knew from experience that only half his arrows were likely to do anything. If the arrows in his quiver were average, only six or maybe seven would work.

Still, he might be lucky, and if he got off good shots, then perhaps he could subdue all eight dragons. So again he put the spurs to his mount.

Just as Sir Fred was almost in range of the nearest dragon, something to his right moved. He looked to the right—there were four more dragons that had just popped in to join the party. Twelve in all, and he was surrounded.

Sir Fred figured that in a few minutes, by one dragon or another, his butt would be barbecued. His along with those of all the travelers.

"Well," Sir Fred said to himself, "it's a good day to die." And he charged.

He drew back his bowstring, shot the first Magic Arrow—and it was perfect. The dragon shrunk smaller and smaller and vanished in a burst of light.

The vanished first dragon left a hole in the ring of the dozen dragons, and Sir Fred took advantage of this to ride straight on.

His tactics did what he hoped. The other eleven dragons now were chasing him.

He turned in his saddle, shot another arrow over his shoulder, and sent another dragon home.

He turned again, shot over his other shoulder, same thing. Now there were only nine dragons after him.

Then he got a bit lucky. He found himself riding into a narrow canyon—too narrow for all the dragons to come in side by side. Now they had to come at him one at a time.

He jumped off his horse and stood with his back to the rocky wall. As each dragon entered the canyon, Sir Fred took careful aim—and shot.

One by one, the dragons dropped. Nine dragons, eight, seven.

With every arrow, he kept waiting for the one that would miss, kept waiting for the dud that would mean his end. But these Magic Arrows were perfect.

Six, five, four, three dragons, two. They vanished as he hit them.

Finally there was only one dragon left—and one Magic Arrow. Would this be the arrow that would miss? Would this be the one with the defective arrowhead that bounced off the dragon's scales? Would this be the Magic Arrow that wasn't magical?

His arm was tired. He pulled back on the bowstring, and as the dragon reared back, preparing to lunge straight at him, he released the arrow and it soared through the air, straight into the dragon's heart. There was a blinding flash of light. The last dragon was gone.

"Yes!" said Sir Fred.

It had been for him a Dozen Dragon Day.

He got back on his horse, rode out of the canyon, was heading back to the castle—when he was lifted into the air, held tightly in the talons of the thirteenth dragon, whom he had not spotted.

Sir Fred prepared for the end. All of the Magic Arrows had worked perfectly, but he had none left. The dragon's jaws opened wide. Sir Fred closed his eyes.

The next thing he remembered, he was flat on his back looking to the sky, and Sir Charlie was there asking him if he was all right.

"What happened? Where's the thirteenth dragon?"

"We got it," said Sir Charlie. "The lookout at the castle saw you were in trouble and we rode hard to get here in time."

Sir Fred got to his feet. There were five other knights with Sir Charlie. Sir Fred breathed a deep sight of relief.

"Let's hear it for teamwork," said Sir Fred.

Sir Fred and Sir Charlie rode back to the castle. Once across the drawbridge, the first thing Sir Fred did was to ask his squire which of the Towers had made the arrows he'd used against the twelve dragons.

His squire told him, and Sir Fred went straight over to Tower Two.

Sir Fred gathered all the arrow-makers of Tower Two, told them the story, and said, "From now on, the only Magic Arrows I will carry with me are those made by Tower Two. For it is your quality that made possible my Twelve Dragon Day."

With this victory came a new color for the arrow-makers of Tower Two. They began to see blue.

The gray and gloom of the place was just about gone. It had almost all the colors now, and their Tower was beginning to look … well, yes, like a rainbow.

13

News of Sir Fred's Twelve-Dragon Day spread throughout the castle. Soon enough, the Duke of Arrows heard about it and he rushed to the Throne Room to tell the King.

" ... and then Sir Fred said he would only carry with him into battle the Magic Arrows made by Tower Two and no others," the duke concluded.

"Is that right?" said the King.

"Yes, sire, the knights now claim that the quality of Tower Two's arrows is far superior to that of the other Towers!"

The King stroked his beard. "Hmmm. But what about the quality of Towers One, Three, and Four? How come their quality isn't just as good as Tower Two's? What are the arrow-makers in Two doing that the others are not?"

Startled, for he did not know the answers, the Duke of Arrows replied, "Well, those are three excellent questions, Your Excellency. Allow me to withdraw to investigate the matter personally and I shall return with the lowdown forthwith!"

"No," said the King, standing from his throne,

"I'll go with you. I want to see this for myself."

Through the gray hallways of the castle went the King and the Duke of Arrows, down dismal staircases and past doorways of rooms where castle workers toiled in the fog. They crossed the courtyard, slowly and carefully, for it was difficult to see where they were going, but then suddenly the fog was gone.

There before them was a stone tower with a big *2* painted on the side of it, and the entire tower was lit up with nearly a full spectrum of colors. It looked as if the tower were in the center of a rainbow, the colors extending out of the roof and curving broadly into the sky.

"Gee," said the Duke of Arrows, "that's pretty neat."

The King, however, was not overly impressed with rainbows. He wanted to know what it was that made Tower Two perform better than the others.

He and the Duke of Arrows went inside, and everybody they saw seemed to have some kind of energy around them. It was the people and the energy they gave off, not the stone Tower, that created all the colors and the light that drove off the fog.

"Your Majesty, Your Dukeship, what can we do for you?" asked Art Halegiver, who was the first to spot them.

"I hear that Tower Two is making the best Magic Arrows in the castle," said the King.

"I wouldn't know about the other Towers," said Art, "but I know that our arrows are now very good and getting better."

"Just how do you know that?" asked the duke.

Art showed them a chart he kept on the shafts he turned out. "I know because we measure our quality and our output, and because we all work together to keep improving."

"And how much extra gold is it costing to produce arrows of such quality?" asked the King.

"Why, it's not costing anything extra," said Art. "In fact, because we now make so few mistakes, because we have so little waste, and because the knights need to shoot fewer arrows to hit the dragons, the castle is actually saving gold with our arrows."

The King clearly was impressed. "How is it that you arrow-makers of Tower Two got so good?"

"Well," said Art, "we just kept trying to improve, we never let anything stop us, and—most important—we got everybody involved. Including the Boss."

"I see," said the King. "And how did you manage to do that?"

"This helped," said Art, showing them *The Zapp! Wizard's Spell Book*. "You see, there was this wizard who dropped by one day, only he wasn't dressed like a wizard—"

"Yes," said the King, "I know the man."

He and the duke thanked Art for his time, then they wandered through the Tower. They talked to the Boss, watched the Zapps flashing back and forth between the arrow-makers, confirmed everything Art had told them. Then they left.

A few paces outside of Tower Two, the fog returned. Thick as soup.

They felt their way over to Tower Three and went inside to have a look around. But here it was all still gray, dark, and gloomy.

"Didn't Tower Two used to be like this?" asked the King.

"Yes, Sire," said the duke. "Indeed, I thought it the darkest and gloomiest of all the towers."

The King talked to a few people in Tower Three, but it soon became clear that there was no teamwork here. And they had no Zapp! to energize them. None of the arrow-makers kept their own measurements, they had no goals, and they did not really know what their quality or their output was. They were all just working the old same way as always.

The King did not tarry long. He dismissed the Duke of Arrows and wandered about the castle for some time, noting that everyplace he went was as dull and fog-filled as Tower Three. Finally, he returned to the Throne Room and sat for some time there, thinking about what he had seen.

Then the King called over one of the castle pages and said, "Remember that wizard who came to see us some time back? Did he leave a way for us to get hold of him?"

"Yes, Your Majesty," said the page, "he left a strange, magical device, the likes of which have never been seen in all of Lamron."

"Go and fetch it immediately."

The page brought the strange device and handed it to the King.

"The wizard claimed this to be something known in

his world as a 'cellular telephone with memory dialer,'" the page explained. "He said that if we ever wanted to contact him, we should press that little silver button right there."

The King touched the button and there was a lot of beeping, followed by a voice that said, "Hello, David D. Ignatius, Zapp! Wizard. How can I help you?"

"This is the King of Lamron. I think we need to get together and talk."

Into Tower Two a while later came a strangely dressed man whom Art Halegiver immediately recognized.

"Hey, Dave! Good to see you!" called Art.

Dave came over, shook hands, and said, "I see you've been using the Zapp! spells. Congratulations, you've done a great job."

"Thanks," said Art, "we keep trying. So what brings you back to Lamron Castle?"

"Just had another meeting with the King," said Dave. "He's commissioned me to teach everyone else in the castle what you folks here in Tower Two have learned. We're going to try to enZapp all the castle workers, from the squires and stablehands to the dukes, and even the King himself."

"That's great news!" said Art. "Listen, Dave, while you're here, I was wondering if you might teach me a new spell for a particular purpose."

"Sure, if I can," said Dave. "What are you trying to do?"

"Well, I came up with this really terrific idea, but I just can't get it accepted," said Art. "Let me tell you what happened. ... "

Some time ago, Art Halegiver was at his workbench, thinking about how he might improve his shaft-turning still further. He happened to look in the corner and saw one of those tiny arrows he'd made, the ones from his "breakthrough" of long ago that he had created by cutting the shafts in half. He had kept one as a souvenir.

All of a sudden, a new idea flashed into his head. The little arrow had failed because it had not fit the knights' bows. But what if it could be shot without a bow? Then the castle might be able to save a pot or two of gold not having to buy as much wood for the shafts. Art became very excited.

Zapp!

He got a long, straight stick of wood, and instead of turning it into an arrow shaft, he drilled out the center so that it became a tube.

In a few days, he showed his friends.

"What the heck is that?" asked Mac.

"I have invented the Blowgun," said Art.

And he proceeded to demonstrate. He inserted the tiny arrow, put the wooden tube to his lips, huffed and puffed, and the little arrow flew across the room and stuck in the wall.

"How about that," said Mac.

Then Art showed the Boss.

"Very interesting," said the Boss. "This may have some possibilities."

So together they showed the Blowgun to the Duke of Arrows, who went wild over it. Just think about all the wood they could save!

The duke immediately approved an order for some sample Blowguns and a limited supply of tiny arrows. When finished, these were delivered to the knights.

And so, proudly, Art Halegiver waited for the Blowgun to catch on. And he waited and waited ... and waited.

Art finally went to the Boss and asked, "What's going on? Whatever happened to my idea with the Blowgun? The Duke of Arrows thought it was a great idea!"

"I don't know," said the Boss. "I haven't heard a thing."

Art went over to the Knights' Keep, and there were the new Blowguns stacked in a far corner gathering dust and cobwebs. The knights were still using the same old bows and arrows. Not one had adopted Art's Blowgun.

"I guess you were plenty disappointed," said Dave, listening with empathy.

"You bet. I don't know what went wrong," said Art. "Even the Duke of Arrows thought it was a great idea. But the knights won't use them! So I want a magic spell that will force the knights to use my Blowgun idea."

"I'm afraid that's impossible," said Dave. "My magic can't force someone to do anything. But, anyway, you don't really need that kind of spell."

"I don't?"

"No, in fact, you already have all the magic you need for this," said Dave. "But in your rush to turn your idea into reality, it seems you forgot to involve a few important people."

"I talked to the Boss," said Art. "I talked to the Duke of Arrows. If they approved, who else did I need?"

"How about the people who have to use your idea, your customers?"

Art suddenly realized why his idea had failed. "I forgot to involve the knights!"

Art and Wizard Dave talked for some time, and afterward Art resolved that he would try again.

He went to the knights and, while invoking the Three Keys Spell, he started asking questions. It turned out that indeed the knights were more than just a little upset that no one had asked them their opinion of the Blowgun before trying to make them use it in the field. After all, they were the ones facing the dragons.

But the knights also had a legitimate practical reason for not using the Blowgun: There was no one in the entire land of Lamron with lungs strong enough to put the little arrows through a dragon's thick scales. They needed a bow with a lot of force and a Blowgun ... well, you get the idea.

In fact, as Art learned in talking to them, this was the root of a major complaint these days among the knights. Used to be that the main reason that knights came home crispy was that they had to hang around and shoot a lot of arrows to get the dragon. If the first arrow didn't work, they had to shoot a second arrow, and if the second didn't work, a third, and so on. The longer the knight had to hang around and shoot, the greater the likelihood that the dragon would win.

But now that arrow quality was very good and getting better, the knights had other worries that had come to the fore.

As Sir Charlie put it, "We appreciate the fact that you arrow-makers have improved quality. And we're not saying, 'Don't worry about quality anymore.' We still want the quality to improve so there are absolutely no failures. It's just that with ninety-nine out of a hundred Magic Arrows working perfectly, we are more concerned with other problems."

"Like what?" asked Art.

It turned out that the current Number One cause of cooked knights was not faulty arrows; it was the fact that the knights had to get in so close to the dragons in order to shoot effectively. What they really needed was not better arrows; they really needed better bows.

Well, Art would have been happy to help them out if he could. There was only one teensy little hang-up. He knew arrows, not bows.

Still, he felt obliged to do something to help. Okay, so maybe the Blowgun had been a flop, but perhaps he could come up with something else that would work. He went to see the Boss.

"Say, Boss, who knows bows?" Art asked. "I mean, it's a big castle, and somebody must know bows."

"Sure, we've got a lot of people who know bows," said the Boss. "But Bob's the best."

"Who?"

"Bob," said the Boss. "Bob-the-Bow-Maker."

"Bob knows bows?"

"Bob knows bows better than anyone. Bob *builds* bows. All the knights use Bob's bows. Why don't you go talk to him?"

Art went to the other side of the castle, found Bob-the-Bow-Maker, and began to explain the Blowgun. But Bob was not much interested in the Blowgun—until Art showed him the new Magic Mini-Arrows. Then Bob became very excited.

"Hey, that's exactly what I've been looking for!" exclaimed Bob.

From under his worktable Bob brought out a strange contraption. It was a long wooden post with a short bow on one end, on the other end some cranks to draw back the string, and a trigger underneath.

Having never seen such a thing before, Art asked, "What the heck is that?"

"I call it the Crossbow," said Bob. "It's twice as powerful as an ordinary bow and a lot more accurate. I invented it over a year ago, but I could never get it to work right because the standard arrows are too big and heavy for it. And I figured I'd never get the arrow-

makers to go along with making smaller arrows.
But if we could combine your idea with mine … "

That was what they decided to do.

But this time, before he did anything else, Art Halegiver did what Wizard Dave had suggested. He thought
about *who should be involved.*

From his mistake with the Blowgun, Art knew that at
or near the top of his list were the knights. If the Crossbow was going to succeed, the knights had to be
involved.

So Art went to the Knights' Keep and said, "What
would you knights think if the arrow-makers could give
you smaller arrows that would be just as effective,
cheaper to make, and lighter for you to carry … plus a
stronger bow that could shoot through the thickest
scales of even the biggest dragons from much greater
range and with much greater accuracy?"

Well, the knights thought this would be terrific.

"Great," said Art. "Then I need a few of you to give
us some time to help develop what I just described."

But Art didn't stop with the knights. He went to the
Boss and explained to her that the knights were highly
enthusiastic about the Crossbow, and asked if she had
any thoughts about how the idea should be developed.

The Boss said, "I'll tell you one group you need to
have involved: the techno-wizards. The Duke of Arrows
really got an earful from the Grand Techno-Wizard over

FROM THE WORKBENCH OF: **ART HALEGIVER**

Tower Two Lamron Castle

**"Involving Others Means ...
Helping People Take Ownership
of an Idea So That They Become
Personally Committed To Its
Development, Implementation,
and Ultimate Success."**

—Wizard Dave

the fact that we tried to implement the Blowgun without the R&D Dungeon knowing about it. And I have to admit, the GTW had a point; the techno-wizards would have spotted the practical limitations of the Blowgun before we spent gold on producing it. So before you go any further, why don't I talk to the GTW and get him to set up a meeting for you with one of his research wizards."

A few days later, Art went down into the R&D Dungeon to meet with a techno-wizard named Stan.

"Crossbow, huh?" said Stan. "Seems to me someone came up with that idea a long time ago."

"Really?" said Art. "Well, what happened to it?"

"Come here," said Stan, "I'll show you."

They went down deeper into the R&D Dungeon to a storeroom way in the subbasement. Stan unlocked the door. Art started to enter and then jumped back, terrified.

"There are ghosts in that room!"

"Not ghosts. Just ghostly visions of dreams and ideas that never came to be," said Stan. "You've got nothing to be afraid of. Step inside."

They went into the room, and Stan began to search among the vaporous visions stored there.

"Let's see. ... Here we have the Magic Lance, the Self-Sharpening Sword, and the Enchanted Catapult," said Stan, pointing out these items. "Oh, and here's my favorite, the Magic Mechanical Super Stallion. Would have galloped at four times the speed of the average horse, if anyone had developed it. Ah, there it is in the corner, the Crossbow."

Art went to touch the vision of the Crossbow, but it was still only an idea and he could not pick it up.

"Hey, Stan, a lot of these seem like they were really great ideas."

"They were great ideas," said Stan. "By the way, we have a couple of other storerooms down here that are filled with ideas that were mediocre or just plain stupid. Ugly critters. Hate to go in those rooms."

"But why isn't the castle using these ideas? The great ones, I mean."

"Because in each case the people who came up with these great ideas thought that was all that they needed to do," said Stan. "They dreamed the dream. They never did much, if anything, to make the dream become reality. They thought that coming up with the idea solved the problem. So their genius and creativity never went anywhere—except here, to the Storeroom of Great Vaporous Visions."

FROM THE WORKBENCH OF: **ART HALEGIVER**

Tower Two Lamron Castle

Just because you've come up with the idea doesn't mean you've solved the problem!

"But, Stan, we *have* a Crossbow. It's more than just an idea," said Art.

"You do?"

"Yes. Bob-the-Bow-Maker invented it and I have the Magic Mini-Arrows to make it work!"

"Then I have to say you're one of the rare ones," said Stan. "You're one of the few who not only come up with an idea, but actually turn the idea into reality. Not many like you. But of course … you're doomed."

"Doomed? Why?"

Stan lowered his voice. "The NIH Monster."

"What's that?"

"Some say it was the perverse aftermath of a failed experiment. Others say it was hatched deliberately by some of the duller techno-wizards to enhance job security," said Stan. "No matter where it came from, the NIH Monster stalks the corridors of the R&D Dungeon—and many other parts of the castle—destroying creativity and wrecking the chances of ideas like yours."

"But what does NIH stand for?"

"Not Invented Here," said Stan.

Sure enough, when Art and Bob presented the Crossbow concept to the Grand Techno-Wizard, midway through their talk, a huge gross gray creature came up through the floor, right behind the GTW's chair. The creature seemed to be made of cast iron. It clamped its hands over the GTW's head. Its iron thumbs plugged the GTW's ears and its fingers spread over the man's head, magically preventing all new thoughts from entering the GTW's mind.

Oddly, the GTW didn't seem to notice.

When Art said, "Look out for that thing behind your chair!" the GTW claimed to see nothing.

"Go on with your presentation," said the GTW irritably. "My time is limited." And when Art and Bob had concluded, the NIH Monster shook the GTW's head and, though the words came out of the GTW's mouth, it was the monster that said, "I can see no merit in pursuing your idea. Besides, you two are not wizards! If the Crossbow had been worth anything, our own techno-wizards would have developed it years ago!"

But by now Art Halegiver had enough Zapp! that even an NIH Monster was not going to stop him.

Instead of giving up, Art got his customers, Sir Fred and the knights, to back him up. Because he had involved the knights early on, they were now convinced that the Crossbow was the way to go, and they were more than ready to hack and slash at anyone who said otherwise.

A week later, there was a second meeting with the GTW. This time, Art Halegiver brought with him not only Bob-the-Bowmaker, but Sir Fred and a number of his biggest and best knights, who brought along some special guests: the Duke of Arrows, the Duke of Bows, and none other than the Duke of Operations.

You see, Art Halegiver, though he was a good man

with good ideas, never would have been able to persuade the dukes to support the Crossbow, not on his own. Because he had the support of the knights, though, the dukes paid attention.

The meeting began and the NIH Monster showed up again. It rose out of the floor and clamped its hands around the GTW's head. But this time, though invisible, Dave the Zapp! Wizard was also in the room—in spirit.

For Art had gone to Dave and got him to teach the knights a much more powerful tactic than hacking and slashing. Dave had taught them the Zapp! spells.

"We knights certainly believe that you and the techno-wizards are brilliant people," said Sir Fred, seeking to maintain the GTW's self-esteem.

Zapp!

"We also believe," Sir Fred continued, "that there are a number of compelling reasons why the R&D Dungeon should reconsider development of the Crossbow."

And as Sir Fred said this, a lightning bolt seemed to unite all of the people Art had brought to the meeting. The lightning suddenly arced across the room—*Zapp!*

The cast-iron body of the NIH Monster suddenly had a gaping hole in it. One of the monster's iron thumbs unplugged itself from an ear of the GTW.

Every time one of the knights or dukes spoke, and showed their support for the Crossbow while invoking the Three Keys Spell, it punched another hole in the cast iron of the NIH Monster, and one by one its fingers curled back, releasing the mind of the Grand Techno-Wizard.

Soon it was revealed that though the NIH Monster appeared invincible, the creature was nothing but a brittle shell around a hollow core.

Finally Art Halegiver closed, saying, "Frankly, we can't develop the Crossbow alone. We would very much like the help of the R&D Dungeon. ..."

Zapp!

At this, the NIH Monster collapsed and became just a pile of chunks on the floor. The GTW said that he would personally follow up on the matter and assign Stan and several top techno-wizards to the Crossbow project.

Zapp!

Art Halegiver and his special team of knights, arrow-makers, bow-makers, and techno-wizards worked hard, but hard work alone was not what kept the Crossbow project moving forward at such a lightning pace. To keep such a diverse and large group of workers in the castle motivated and moving forward, in spite of setbacks and problems, took a lot of Zapp!

Even after they had a working prototype, the real work had only begun. One of the most important things they did was to take a critical look at their invention and ask themselves, What kind of difficulties are people likely to have using it?

From this, they deduced that the knights were not trained to use the Crossbow. So the team made plans to have training sessions at the Knights' Keep. They also had the knights take the Crossbow into the field and test it. This way, they discovered that the Crossbow was heavier than the bow and would be harder to aim. So they developed a special sling to help the knights deal with the weight.

Then they had to get the Crossbow into production. With the Magic Mini-Arrows, most of the tools and processes of arrow-making had to be adapted. And the bow-makers had to set up a whole new process to make the Crossbow itself.

During this time, Wizard Dave worked with them to make the Crossbow team as enZapped as it could be. He taught them a lot of little tips and tricks to keep the Zapp! flowing freely and smoothly.

Finally the early Crossbows and the Magic Mini-Arrows were ready for field use.

The first time Sir Fred was called to battle to face a dragon with the new Crossbow, he found that he could stop half a mile away, shoot, and dispatch the monster without ever coming in range of the dragon's fire breath.

Within a few moons, the superiority of the Crossbow over the conventional bow was obvious. Not only did the safety record of the knights improve dramatically, but their hit ratio went up as well. With the Crossbow, the knights did not have to spend time galloping around the dragon dodging claws and fire breath and snapping teeth to get close enough to shoot. They could ride up, get rid of the dragon with one easy shot, and ride on to the next call.

FROM THE WORKBENCH OF: **ART HALEGIVER**

Tower Two Lamron Castle

Team Tips from Wizard Dave ...

- Write a charter or mission statement: keep it posted in a common team area.

- Write clear goals everyone agrees to; refer to them at the start of each meeting.

- Define individual roles and responsibilities and ensure each is clear and meaningful.

- Revise roles and short-term goals as projects and tasks change.

- Try to balance individual needs and skills with team roles.

- Establish procedures for solving conflicts.

- Don't interrupt; let each other complete a thought when speaking.

- Clarify information you don't understand.

- Touch base with each other between team meetings.

- Let everyone have his or her say before making a decision.

- Encourage and build on others' ideas and initiative.

- Accept and give constructive feedback.

- Confront disagreements openly.

- Don't move ahead until the team reaches consensus.

- Don't let resentment build up and cause an explosion.

- Give the team leader immediate, constructive, and honest feedback. (Leaders are more secure if feedback is out in the open, even if feelings are negative.)

- Involve leader in key events and decisions (even if team members are mostly self-sufficient).

Pretty soon, all of the knights had switched to Crossbows. No other castle in the whole Magic World had such an effective means of countering the increasingly grave dragon menace.

FROM THE WORKBENCH OF: **ART HALEGIVER**

Tower Two Lamron Castle

The Only Good Idea
Is an Implemented Idea …
That Stays Implemented!

Almost as important was a fresh awareness that came about because of the Crossbow project. Never before had so many different groups within Lamron Castle worked together so successfully. Through the magical energy of Zapp!, they began to sense a connection between one another.

They were not just arrow-makers or bow-makers or knights or dukes or techno-wizards. They were dragon fighters, every one of them, no matter what the specific job.

And with this realization came sight of the final color of the rainbow … purple.

With Dave the Zapp! Wizard teaching all the other towers and dungeons and keeps of the castle the spells they needed to work together harmoniously, they gained the full spectrum—red, orange, yellow, green, blue, and purple—the full rainbow.

FROM THE WORKBENCH OF: **ART HALEGIVER**

Tower Two Lamron Castle

We Are Not Just Arrow-makers, or Knights, or Dukes, or Wizards. We are Dragon Fighters All with a Common Mission. We Need the Magic from Each Other to Win.

14

The Crossbow was a tremendous advancement, a true breakthrough, not just technically, but because of the Zapp! that helped bring it about. Yet this is not where our story ends.

One morning, the King called all of the workers of the castle into the courtyard and announced, "The Dragon Moon finally has passed! I wish to congratulate you all! Because of your many efforts, the dragons have been held at bay! At least for now."

At lunch, Mac, Art, and Wendy began to wonder. What did the King mean when he said, "For now"?

After they ate, they went and talked to the Boss about this.

"I asked the duke about this myself," said the Boss. "What the King meant is that nothing ever stays the same. Today the crisis has passed. We are holding our own. But the dragons are always getting stronger and smarter—and so are the other castles. I just saw an announcement from the Duke of Marketing that the other castles have heard about the Crossbow and they're already developing their own. And even though we've now matched the prices of the neighboring castles, what will happen if those castles cut their prices even further? Will we ever find a way to win back the Lamronian citizens who left us for the likes of Castle Colossal? So, as for tomorrow, who knows?"

And there was another fear circulating through Tower Two—as well as Towers One, Three, and Four. It was a quiet, seldom-spoken fear almost as scary as the dragons themselves.

Mac was one of the first to express it: "You know, I was wondering what we're all going to do when the arrow-makers in the other towers improve as much as we have."

"If they keep improving," said Wendy, "we'll have more than enough high-quality arrows to defeat the dragons, no matter how many dragons show up."

"Yeah," said Mac, "that's what worries me."

"I don't follow you."

"I think we might have too many arrow-makers for the arrow-making that needs to be done," said Mac.

"I hadn't thought about that," said Wendy. "I guess it's up to the King and the dukes and the bosses to think about those things."

"Well," said Mac, "I believe that maybe it's time we *all* started to think about these things."

Mac brought up the issue before the other arrow-makers of Tower Two. And in some ways this was the toughest problem they had ever faced.

"Now that the crisis has passed," said Fernanda, "why don't we go back to doing things the old way?"

"Fernanda, there is no way we can go back to yesterday," Mac said. "We have to keep moving forward."

"But what if it means we can't be arrow-makers?" asked Gramps. "What are we going to do?"

"Then," said Mac, "we have to find new ways for ourselves to bring in gold for the castle."

"But arrow-making is all I know!"

"Wait a minute!" said Mac. "A few moons ago, you would have said that twine-tying is all you know. But with Zapp! and all the changes we have made around here, you now know every job in the Tower. We have all learned how to improve. Let's keep going! Let's keep learning! Let's find new ways to help the castle's customers!"

Meanwhile, the arrow-makers were not the only people in the castle thinking about the future. The dukes were thinking about it as well.

You see, the dukes were no dummies. When they were not pressured by the King and one another into concocting Quick Improvement Programs, the dukes often demonstrated that they were smart, that they knew a lot, and that they could get things done.

On one of his visits Wizard Dave had set up a workshop in the castle and with the help of several apprentices had taught the dukes all of the Zapp! spells that the arrow-makers had learned—and a few others reserved for those with the authority of dukes and kings.

One morning, several dukes—the Duke of Arrows, the Duke of Marketing, and the Duke of Operations— were seated around a table in one of the great halls of the Inner Castle, discussing the future.

"With the passing of the Dragon Moon," said the Duke of Arrows, "and the dragon menace increasingly under control, we need to seek out new opportunities."

"New opportunities?" asked the Duke of Operations. "For what?"

"Opportunities to be of service to the citizens of Lamron," said the Duke of Arrows.

"I agree!" said the Duke of Marketing. "And the quicker the better. I just got a report that Castle Colossal is turning its south wing into a theme park! And Count Discount is moving into fashion apparel! This castle must prepare new goods and services to make the Lamronians prosperous, or once again we risk losing citizens to the competition!"

"But we don't know anything about theme parks and fashion apparel," said the Duke of Operations. "Lamron Castle was set up to fight dragons, and that's what we should stick with."

"This is undoubtedly wise," said the Duke of Marketing. "But there are many related ventures into which we could expand."

"And who will perform the tasks required of these new ventures?" asked the Duke of Operations.

"My arrow-makers," said the Duke of Arrows.

The Duke of Operations shot him a highly skeptical look.

"In a few moons, there will be a surplus of talented arrow-makers relative to the demand for Magic Mini-Arrows. It makes no sense to have all of them keep improving arrow production—and very good sense to apply their energies to ventures that the citizens will deem to be of great value."

"But they're just arrow-makers!" complained the Duke of Operations, as if to say, "And that's all they'll ever be."

In fact, there was a bit of truth to this. There were arrow-makers like Dilbert Dooley, who was probably going to be a head-shaper's helper (or something similar) for the rest of his career. Yet, as the Duke of Arrows knew by now, there also were many arrow-makers who were capable of much more.

"I think you may have a surprise coming," the Duke of Arrows told the Duke of Operations, "because I've asked several of the arrow-makers—and a few others as well—to join us today."

He gave a nod to one of his assistant dukes, who opened the door and admitted Art, Mac, and Wendy. Behind them came Sir Fred of the knights and Stan from the R&D Dungeon.

"These three arrow-makers came to me recently and asked if they could become involved in our efforts," said the Duke of Arrows. "So why don't we cast the Inter-ACTION Spell and explore some alternatives."

"Excellent suggestion," said the Duke of Marketing. *Zapp!*

They began by stating what they wanted to accomplish and why it was important. What new ventures could the arrow-makers help develop that would provide goods or services of substantial value to the Lamronian citizens?

"Let's clarify some details," said Wendy. "First of all, how many arrow-makers would be available?"

"As many as fifty percent," said the Duke of Arrows.

"Do most Lamronians have gold that they would be willing to spend on things other than dragon protection?" asked Art.

"Certainly. Pots full, some of them," said the Duke of Marketing. "But the citizens are not willing to part with their gold unless they feel they are getting something valuable in return."

"Okay," said Mac. "What might we make or do that they would value?"

Here they began to develop ideas and possibilities.

"Well," said Sir Fred, "I don't know how the arrow-makers would fit into this, but many of the citizens I have rescued would very much like to see faster response time. I have a hunch that at least a few might even pay extra for faster service."

"Here's another possibility," said Stan. "Down in the Storerooms of Vaporous Visions are many great ideas that would be of benefit to the citizenry. Some, I believe, could be developed rather quickly."

"Why haven't we developed these ideas before now?" asked the Duke of Marketing.

"For one thing, we've been too busy fighting dragons," said Stan. "For another, we never had enough Zapp! for groups of people like ourselves to get behind some of these ideas, fight the gremlins and the NIH Monsters, and make these visions become real."

"Speaking of visions," said the Duke of Operations, "what about the Far-Out Lands?"

At the mention of the Far-Out Lands, everyone around the table flinched.

"But ... but no one has ever seen the Far-Out Lands!" said the Duke of Arrows.

"How far out are the Far-Out Lands?" asked Wendy.

"They lie over the mountain and across the Big Waters," said Sir Fred. "And I have long thought someone ought to go check them out. Why don't I ask the King if he will allow us to dispatch some knights-errant to go see what's there."

Now they began to decide on some actions.

The Duke of Marketing would arrange for a survey of the citizenry to find out how much they truly valued faster service.

Stan would go through the storerooms and select some of the more promising Vaporous Visions, based on how quickly they could be developed and how much gold they might bring in.

Sir Fred would seek permission from the King to explore the Far-Out Lands.

And Art, Mac, and Wendy would canvass their coworkers to see what talents and skills they possessed beyond arrow-making, and who would be motivated to try a new venture.

Then they would meet again to move on to further stages.

Zapp!

Now, the trick of new ventures is to move quickly, wisely, and well. The dukes suspected (correctly) that if the development was dragged out, either the King would grow impatient and lose interest, or the other castles would steal away citizens by completing the venture first. So the dukes made every effort to keep things humming along.

Just a few moons later, in the Throne Room, they assembled to present their plans to the King and seek his approval to proceed. Gathered there were knights, arrow-makers, dukes, and wizards.

"Your Majesty," said the Duke of Operations, "we are here today to present a four-part plan that will make productive use of all of the castle's resources, including our many fine workers; will improve the lives and general prosperity of all Lamronians; will win back many former citizens who have settled in other kingdoms; and will, by the way, put a heck of a lot more gold into the Treasure Chest."

"I'm interested," said the King. "Especially in that last part. Proceed!"

This was the plan:

The four towers that had exclusively made arrows would now pursue different gold-earning ventures. Each would have its own mission, measurements, and goals.

Tower One would be dedicated to traditional dragon fighting and would continue to improve the quality and output of Magic Mini-Arrows.

Tower Two would become headquarters of a group that would improve the response times of the knights and pay for itself through extra services.

"You see, Your Majesty," said Wendy, "we have discovered that the knights spend eighty percent of their time in the field not fighting dragons, but galloping back and forth to the Castle. This is hard on the horses and a general waste of time, but necessary because the knights need to resupply themselves with Magic Mini-Arrows and other provisions."

"We plan to reduce travel time for the knights," said Mac, "and increase citizen satisfaction by establishing way-points at certain points in the countryside. Former arrow-makers like myself will go out into the field each day and stock these way points with Magic Mini-Arrows and other provisions, like hay for horses, so that the knights can stay on patrol in the field and respond to dragon sightings much more quickly."

"No other castle in the whole wide Magic World has such a system," said the Duke of Marketing. "We estimate the average response time will drop from half an hour to five minutes."

The King nodded sagely. "Fine. What about Tower Three?"

"Observe, Your Majesty," said Stan, the techno-wizard, and he proceeded to spill a cup of coffee onto the King's red carpet. He then took from out of his sleeve a long stick with a glittery star on the end. "Permit me to introduce the Magic Cleaning Wand."

Stan waved the wand over the spilled coffee and in a jiffy the red carpet was clean again.

"Amazing," said the King.

"This wand will do a thousand and one household chores, and we can have them in stores across the Land of Lamron before the holidays," said Stan.

"Who's going to make them?" asked the King.

"I will," said Art Halegiver. "Myself and my team of arrow— er, wand-makers. We will set up shop in Tower Three to make and service these Magic Cleaning Wands and many other fine products that Stan and the techno-wizards will continue to develop."

"Very good," said the King. "And Tower Four?"

"Your Majesty," said Sir Fred, "the knights we dispatched to explore the Far-Out Lands have returned with important news. They have ridden far and wide and discovered that over the mountains and across the Big Waters are many lands where dragons roam freely and cause great misery among the inhabitants."

"No kidding. Are there a lot of dragons?" asked the King.

"Hordes," said Sir Fred. "And many other monsters besides."

"Have they no castles, no knights, no Magic Arrows to protect them?"

"None, Sire," said Sir Fred. "Thus I plan to use Tower Four to train a new corps of knights and arrow-makers. Our mission will be to adapt Lamronian dragon-fighting tools and tactics to the unique needs of those regions and to expand our dragon-fighting services to help the Far-Out citizens."

"Excellent!" cried the King. "You have my whole-hearted approval! Let's do it! Let's clobber Count Dis-count and Castle Colossal before they know what's hit them! Let's make it happen!"

Zapp!

So began a great period in Lamron Castle's history.

Among the four teams, there was a place for all the arrow-makers, even though many of them were no longer making arrows.

In time, Lamron Castle had beaten all the other cas-tles with respect to fast service and excellent new prod-ucts.

Because of the discovery of dragons in the Far-Out Lands and the sale of much-needed services to their cit-izens, the castle even had to run want ads in the *The Lamron News* to hire more Lamronians.

With continuing improvements, *Dragon Digest* came to rate Lamron Castle once again as the standard of excellence in dragon protection.

And, over the long run, the Land of Lamron became peaceful and prosperous once more, with everybody earning more than enough gold to live a happy life.

Just as important, Art, Mac, Wendy, and the other castle workers found that because of the Zapp! Magic created by Dave's spells, life was satisfying not just after hours at nighttime and on the weekends, but while they were at work as well.

As Wizard Dave began to teach his spells to everybody, the bigger bolts of Zapp! began to flash. They flashed not only between people, but between teams and between towers—and with such frequency that the entire castle lit up. It was not just a bolt of Zapp! here and a flash of Zapp! there, but continuous lightning.

The fog lifted. The castle brightened. And in the light of Zapp!, many of the walls and battlements within the castle were seen for what they were: unnecessary illusions. They went away and the castle began to look less like a fortress and more like a great place to do good work.

The Zapp! became not just one color or several colors, but all colors combined, and more than a rainbow. It became like pure daylight.

Now, the King, of course, became very proud of all of the castle workers and rightly so.

Often, the King would go up to one of the higher towers and watch in amazement as the Zapp! flowed from one castle worker to another. The King himself even learned the Zapp! spells from Wizard Dave and did whatever he could to increase the Zapp! in Lamron Castle.

But for some time, the King had been hearing from many sources the story of how Zapp! first began to flash many moons before over in Tower Two. Who had been responsible, he wondered, for the early successes that ultimately saved the entire castle? He asked the former Boss of Tower Two, who now had been promoted and was the Duchess of New Products.

"Art, Mac, and Wendy," replied the Duchess. "In fact, if Your Majesty would consider a suggestion … "

"By all means," said the King.

"Your Majesty really ought to give those three some sort of special praise. For though all the castle workers deserve credit for what has taken place, it was Art, Mac, and Wendy who began it all."

And Dave the Zapp! Wizard concurred. He told the King the story of how Art Halegiver had shot the dragon that had nearly gobbled him up and how Art and his two friends had pressed him for the Three Keys Spell that had started it all.

So one day, the King invited Art, Mac, and Wendy to join him for lunch.

They went to the highest floor of the King's Keep, where a great banquet had been spread in their honor.

"So tell me," said the King, munching a breadstick, "what do you think personally of all this Zapp! going around nowadays? I mean, it's done a lot for the castle, but what has it done for you three personally?"

"It's done a great deal for me," said Art Halegiver. "You know, before all this started, I used to be bored. I didn't like my job. I wanted to quit. And now I feel like I'm in charge of my job. I never get bored because I'm always looking for ways to make my job better. My job keeps changing, but I feel that I have a voice in how that change takes place. Zapp! is great stuff."

"What I like," said Mac, "is that we made life better not only for ourselves, but for a lot of other people. We may never get rid of the dragons completely, but now we can control them, rather than the other way around. I'm proud of what we've been able to do."

"This is what I like best," said Wendy. And she took from her purse a letter from her father. Enclosed with the letter was a story from *Dragon Digest* touting Lamron Castle as once again the very best in the whole wide Magic World. The letter said that Wendy's parents were selling their place near Castle Colossal and moving back to Lamron.

Finally, we feel confident that Lamron Castle will do the job right, her father wrote, *and what happened long ago will not happen again.*

After lunch, as Art, Mac, and Wendy were about to go back to work, the King instead took them down to the Throne Room. And there was David D. Ignatius, Zapp! Wizard.

"The King and I have prepared something special for you," said Dave. "For being the first to learn the Zapp! spells, and for showing leadership before your coworkers, we have decided that you should be the first to receive a special recognition."

Whereupon, Dave opened his briefcase, offered it to the King, and the King bestowed upon each of the three a big golden medal on a rainbow ribbon.

And on the face of the medal, it read: "Hero."

"These medals will now be the highest awards Lamron

Castle will bestow," said the King. "We hope that every-one in the castle will eventually earn one."

"I don't know if we deserve these," said Mac.

"Yeah, we're not heroes," said Wendy.

"We were just doing our jobs," said Art Halegiver.

And Dave said, "That's what all heroes say. You see, a true hero is not just someone who accomplishes an extraordinary deed one time. The real heroes are the people who work together at ordinary jobs, struggling day after day, often against great odds and indifference, to make the world around them better and better and better. That is what you have accomplished. You are true heroes."

And then with all the Zapp! circulating in the charged air of the castle, there was a great clap of thunder and a brilliant flash of lightning—*Zapp!* When Art, Mac, and Wendy looked at their medals, they found that the inscription had changed.

It now read …

You probably don't live in Lamron. Or in any magic land. The place where you work might not even look like a castle.

Instead, you probably work in some job at a Normal organization, be it corporate or public, for profit or not.

And you probably have to work with Normal people (well, at least they claim to be).

Even if you are freelance, roving solo and offering your services to castles—er, organizations—far and wide, your job is the same as everyone else's.

You are a dragon fighter.

We are all dragon fighters of one kind or another. That's how we earn our gold.

Whether you are wizard, knight, arrow-maker, or king, your job is to fight dragons that afflict the people whom your castle serves.

Now, the beasts of the moment may not look like dragons—with scales, a tail, teeth, hot breath, and all that—but that's what they are.

There are dragons of hunger, dragons of thirst. Dragons of darkness, dragons of disease. Dragons of ignorance, dragons of the unknown. Late dragons, dull dragons, dragons of mistakes. You got a problem, you can bet there is a dragon behind it somewhere.

The dragons are real. They are whatever block human beings from a better life. Make no mistake, the dragons will have us for dinner if somebody doesn't fight them.

People know this. They are not stupid. That's why

they part with their hard-earned gold to fight the dragons they can't fight on their own.

And if our particular castle, company, city, or country doesn't do the job, another will. There is always
another out there trying to do a better job.

But no hero, not even a Normal hero, can fight the
dragons alone. There are too many of them. The monsters are too big.

We need to fight dragons together.

We need to learn the magic that will let us work
together, that will give us the Zapp! to keep getting better at what we do, and keep the dragons away.

These days, we all need to become HeroZ.

The Zapp! Wizard's
Spell Book

Learn these spells.
They will serve you well.

The Zapp! Wizard's Spell Book

Three Keys Spell

Cast the Three Keys Spell
by Behaving Toward Others
According to These Principles:

1. **Maintain or enhance self-esteem.**

2. **Listen and respond with empathy.**

3. **Ask for help and encourage involvement.**

**Apply Ample *Zapp!* From the
Three Keys in All interactions—
Especially When Casting
the Other Spells in this Book.**

The Zapp! Wizard's Spell Book

The ACTION Spell

Use to Solve Problems
and Implement Solutions

To Cast the ACTION Spell:

1. *A*ssess Situation and Define Problem.

2. Determine *C*auses.

3. *T*arget Solutions and Develop Ideas.

4. *I*mplement Ideas.

5. Make it an *ON*going Process.

IMPORTANT: Be Sure to *Involve Others*
While Casting Each Step of This Spell!

The Zapp! Wizard's Spell Book

The InterACTION Spell

Based on the same magic as the ACTION Spell, the InterACTION Spell can be cast in all kinds of practical discussions, whether one-on-one, or in group meetings with many people. It will work in any practical situation in which participants need to stay on track and arrive at a decision with others.

To Cast:

1. **Open with what is to be accomplished and why it is important.**

2. **Clarify the details.**

3. **Develop ideas.**

4. **Agree on actions.**

5. **Close with review decisions and set appropriate follow-up.**

The Zapp! Wizard's Spell Book

The Master Spell of Support

Spell #1: Coaching Spell

Spell #2: Guide-Through-Feedback Spell

Spell #3: Encouragement Spell

The Zapp! Wizard's Spell Book

Coaching Spell

Part I
To Be Cast by Experienced People
When Inexperienced People Are Beginning
New Tasks and Ventures.

1. Ask Questions.

2. Listen for Understanding.

3. Share Knowledge, Experience.

Part 2
To Be Cast by Those in Need of Coaching
When Beginning a New Task
or When Difficulties and Fellings of Uncertainty
Arise.

1. Share Your Needs and Problems.

2. Listen.

3. Ask Questions.

The Zapp! Wizard's Spell Book

The Guide-Through-Feedback Spell
To help people keep going in the right direction

Positive Feedback

★ **Tell exactly what was done right.**

★ **Explain what made this action "right."**

Improvement Feedback

★ **Tell what could have been done better.**

★ **Explain your reasons why.**

★ **Provide a suggestion on how to improve.**

The Zapp! Wizard's Spell Book

The Encouragement Spell

People Need Encouragement to Gain Energy
for Continued Improvement

To Cast Encouragement:

Give Praise When Someone Has Done Well.

★ **Be honest.**

★ **Be specific.**

★ **Be timely.**

★ **With partial success, praise what went well.**

★ **Don't overdo it.**

★ **Celebrate success.**

The Zapp! Wizard's Spell Book

Magic Brew to Enhance Acceptance When Presenting Ideas to Bosses

Start With: 1 Good Idea.

Include Satisfactory Answers to the Following:

★ **Which organizational goals or values are supported by my ideas?**

★ **What are the benefits and costs of my idea?**

★ **What incentive will the Boss have for saying "yes"?**

★ **What will the Boss's objections most likely be?**

★ **What can I say in response if the Boss voices those objections?**

★ **What are some alternatives if the Boss won't buy my idea "as is"?**

Turn the concepts of **HeroZ** *into reality!*

Now that you've read **HeroZ,** *what are you going to do next?*

Sure, *HeroZ* is a fable, but, in fact, the concepts in *HeroZ* are quite real. They come from decades of research conducted by Development Dimensions International (DDI)—a leading provider of training and consulting services. Our research has lead to the creation of one of the most dynamic training technologies ever to hit the marketplace—**Techniques for an Empowered Workforce®.**

Developed under the leadership of *HeroZ* author William C. Byham, **Techniques** was designed to help organizations succeed by creating heroes at all levels of an organization.

The principles of *HeroZ* are already becoming reality for thousands of organizations that are using the **Techniques** training system and other services provided by DDI. Organizations all over the world are changing dramatically—involving and empowering their employees, building teams, and improving everything along the way.

The results have been nothing short of phenomenal. Cost savings. Reduced turnover. Quality awards and other forms of national recognition. But most of all, motivated, team-thinking heroes whose new spirit of involvement is clearly helping their organizations succeed!

Our research has revealed that there are five steps to creating an organization of heroes:

Step 1 **Create and build teams.** The **Team Action®** series of Techniques explores the nature of teamwork and builds skills—including important meeting skills—for team leaders and members.

Step 2 **Build personal empowerment skills.** The learning unit of **Interaction®** address the interpersonal skills people need to form collaborative relationships that help them solve quality problems, address service issues, and handle job conflicts. **Service Plus®** develops skills customer-contact employees need to meet or *exceed* customers' expectations.

Step 3 **Turn continuous quality improvement from theory into practice.** Learning units from **Taking Action®** teach the importance of quality and continuous improvement on the job and build skills that enable your workforce to fully imprememt their good ideas!

Step 4 **Create a high-involvement culture.** Leaders who support and model empowerment are essential to creating and sustaining a high-involvement culture. This is accomplished through several DDI programs:

> **Interaction Management** introduces empowering leadership concepts and strengthens empowerment skills (which are portrayed in the international bestseller, *Zapp! The Lightning of Empowerment*). They learn how to encourage initiative, foster involvement and collaboration, and coach for enhanced performance.

> **Targeted Management** develops leadership essentials managers need to communicate the vision for empowerment, establish an environment of trust, and lead groups toward high-quality decisions.

> **Strategies for High-involvement Leadership** help leaders learn to manage successfully in an empowering environment. They learn to focus on a shared vision, champion innovation, and develop a strong sense of interdependence, trust, and partnership.

Finally, perhaps the most critical part of creating an empowered organization is hiring people who have the skills and motivation to be empowered or empowering. **Targeted Selection** is a legally credible interviewer training program that helps organizations make smart hiring and promotion decisions.

For more information about the programs and services available through Development Dimensions International, please call our Marketing Information Center at 1-800-933-4463 between 8:oo a.m. and 5:00 p.m. EST.

Also, we'd love to hear from you about your reactions to *HeroZ*. Send your letter to William C. Byham, President/CEO, Development Dimensions International, 1225 Washington Pike, Bridgeville, PA, 15017, or via the following e-mail addresses: Internet Website at info@ddiworld.com and the Microsoft Network at ddi@msn.com.

About the Authors

WILLIAM C. BYHAM is president and CEO of Development Dimensions International, a world leader in providing human resource training programs and services. He is also the author of the national bestseller *ZAPP! The Lightning of Empowerment*. He lives in Pittsburgh, Pennsylvania.

JEFF COX coauthored *ZAPP!* and is also the coauthor of two other popular business books, *The Quadrant Solution* and *The Goal*. He lives in Murrysville, Pennsylvania.